The Patent Office

The
Patent
Office

Stacy V. Jones

PRAEGER PUBLISHERS
New York • Washington • London

PRAEGER PUBLISHERS
111 Fourth Avenue, New York, N.Y. 10003, U.S.A.
5, Cromwell Place, London S.W. 7, England

Published in the United States of America in 1971
by Praeger Publishers, Inc.

© 1971 by Praeger Publishers, Inc.

This book is No. 29 in the series
Praeger Library of U.S. Government Departments and Agencies

Library of Congress Catalog Card Number: 79–101666

Printed in the United States of America

To my wife,
MARGARET CRAHAN JONES

Preface

In its 180 years, the United States Patent Office has granted protection on more than three and a half million inventions—some of them milestones in industrial progress, many of them minor improvements on what was already known, and a few of them highly intriguing, such as concrete fences with holes for birds' nests, and ballpark bases with microphones to let the fans hear players argue.

During their terms, all these patents have given their owners at least a chance to profit. To promote science and the useful arts, the Constitution empowered Congress to grant inventors, for limited times, the exclusive rights to their discoveries. Today the many employed inventors give their companies title to their patents and benefit through the payroll. When a patent expires, the technology goes into the public domain for anybody to use. The government's appeal to self-interest, with restricted monopoly as reward, stimulates ingenuity and offers advantages to the inventor, industry, and society at large.

The center of the American patent system, the Patent Office, is small as federal agencies go, but its work is important and colored with romance. Its task is not easy: a constant struggle to cope with the swelling volume of patent applications and the growing intricacy of invention. The examiners must try to know everything that has gone before, so that the patents they award will remain valid under expert attack. To an outsider, the staff appears to be doing its best with a difficult job.

This book is an effort to give the student, the prospective careerist, and the general reader an idea of the Patent Office's history, organization, operation, and place in the nation, with some account of its troubles and accomplishments. Although there are constant changes in detail, patents are being granted pretty much as they were in 1836, and a picture of Patent Office operations drawn today is likely to be generally true tomorrow.

The patent system is held in high esteem by industry, its chief beneficiary, although its friends and critics agree that improvements can be made in its domestic service and in its international relations—aimed at the distant goal of a universal patent, valid throughout the world.

One thing that remains constant is the fascinating variety of inventions. This observer, after many years of writing about patents, still looks forward to the disclosures he will find every Tuesday in the Patent Office *Official Gazette*. Sometimes he is asked whether he is a patent lawyer or an engineer, but the answer on both counts is no. Indeed, ignorance seems to pay, because what interests the lay reporter is likely to interest the mythical average reader and to facilitate the translation of technical idiom into everyday talk.

For this book, the writer has drawn on many expert sources, and must broadcast his thanks. Isaac Fleischmann, Ernest A. Norwig, and Rene D. Tegtmeyer, among others in the Patent Office, have been generous with their time, as has Harvey J. Winter of the Department of State. Acknowledgments are due officials and patent counsel of numerous other federal agencies, the staffs of the congressional committees, and private organizations, particularly the PTC Research Institute of George

Washington University. The helpful lawyers have included (besides the late Henry R. Ashton) Paul L. Gomory, L. James Harris, Alan Latman, and Joseph Rossman, as well as two former Commissioners of Patents: David L. Ladd (whose Patent Commissioner's "dream" provides a fitting conclusion to this volume) and Robert C. Watson. And acknowledgment is made to the *New York Times* (which has carried this writer's patent column since 1952) and *Science Digest* for permission to incorporate or paraphrase certain material written for them.

STACY V. JONES

Falls Church, Virginia
August, 1970

Contents

xi

Tables and Charts

A section of photographs follows page 84.

The Patent Office

I

Fuel for the Fire of Genius

The United States Patent Office is of Anglo-Saxon descent. Although England seems to have borrowed the idea of monopolies for inventions from Continental Europe, the American patent system derives from English practice going back to the reign of Elizabeth I.

Our patent today is a grant of limited monopoly, giving the owner the right to exclude others from making, using, or selling the protected invention for seventeen years. Originally letters patent, or *literae patentes,* were royal grants of commercial rights, usually made to encourage commerce and industry but sometimes to gratify a favorite. In the early fourteenth century, King Edward III awarded grants to foreign weavers to induce them to settle in England. In 1440

3

John of Shiedame got letters patent to import a newly invented process of manufacturing salt.

The Republic of Venice encouraged the development of printing and other arts, as early as the fifteenth century, by various concessions. The Doge of Venice granted Galileo a 20-year patent in 1594 on "a machine for raising water and irrigating land with small expense and great convenience." Some years earlier, in 1559, the second year of Elizabeth's reign, Giacopo Acontio, an Italian, applied for a patent on certain furnaces and "wheel-machines." His argument, that others would copy them to his loss unless he were protected and that "those who by searching have found out things useful to the public should have some fruits of their rights and labors," is credited with inauguration of an English policy of rewarding inventors with patents for their discoveries. He shortly received a pension of £50 a year and, in time, the patent itself.

Patents were a royal prerogative, and many of those granted to favorites were not for inventions. Sir Walter Raleigh was given the right to license tavern keepers and to take over land abroad. In the hands of courtiers, such patents became a means of plunder. The House of Commons investigated the abuses and in 1624 adopted a Statute of Monopolies, but it was many years before the system was entirely freed from royal whim.

THE AMERICAN SYSTEM

The intrinsic right of an inventor to profit from his invention was recognized by law for the first time anywhere when President George Washington signed the Patent Act of April 10, 1790.

The history of U.S. Patent Office practice and operation falls in three general periods. For the first three years patents were granted under an examination system. Examination, carrying a presumption of validity, has now become traditional and distinguishes American procedure from that in many countries abroad. By 1793 the work had become a burden to busy officials, and the law was amended to substitute a registration system, in which applications were filed without examination, and rival claimants were left to settle their differences somehow. Again, in 1836, examination was resumed, and a new law laid the basis for the modern system. Although there have been many amendments to the patent law since then, and two general revisions, the principles have remained unaltered. Even the still pending patent "reform" bill, based on the report of the President's Commission on the Patent System (Appendix C), has been whittled down to embody relatively minor changes.

The 1790 law put the burden of examining patent applications, and the models that accompanied most of them, upon a board consisting of the Secretary of State (then Thomas Jefferson), the Secretary of War (Henry Knox), and the Attorney General (Edmund Randolph). They were authorized to issue a patent "if they shall deem the invention or discovery sufficiently useful or important" and to fix the term at not more than fourteen years.

The first United States patent was granted July 31, 1790, to Samuel Hopkins of Philadelphia for a method of making potash, useful in soap production. The records were burned in the disastrous Patent Office fire of 1836, and the Patent Office remained without a copy until 1955, when the original was found in the possession of the Chicago Historical Society. The text follows:

[Seal]   THE UNITED STATES.

To all to whom these Presents shall come. Greeting.

WHEREAS Samuel Hopkins of the City of Philadelphia and State of Pensylvania [sic] hath discovered an Improvement, not known or used before such Discovery, in the making of Pot-ash and Pearl-ash by a new Apparatus and Process; that is to say, in the making of Pearl-ash 1st by burning the raw Ashes in a Furnace, 2^{d} by dissolving and boiling them when so burnt in Water, 3rd by drawing off and settling the Ley, 4th by boiling the Ley into Salts which then are the true Pearl-ash; and also in the making of Pot-ash by fluxing the Pearl-ash so made as aforesaid; which Operation of burning the raw Ashes in a Furnace, preparatory to their Dissolution and boiling in Water, is new, leaves little Residuum; and produces a much greater Quantity of Salt: These are therefore in pursuance of the Act, entitled "An Act to promote the Progress of useful Arts," to grant to the said Samuel Hopkins, his Heirs, Administrators and Assigns, for the Term of fourteen Years, the sole and exclusive Right and Liberty of using, and vending to others the said Discovery, of burning the raw Ashes previous to their being dissolved and boiled in Water, according to the true Intent and Meaning of the Act aforesaid. IN TESTIMONY whereof I have caused these Letters to be made patent, and the Seal of the United States to be hereunto affixed. Given under my Hand at the City of New York this thirty-first Day of July in the Year of our Lord one thousand seven hundred & Ninety.

G. WASHINGTON

City of New York July 31st 1790.–

I do hereby certify that the foregoing Letters Patent were delivered to me in pursuance of the Act, entitled "An Act to promote the Progress of useful Arts"; that I have examined the same and find them conformable to the said Act.

EDM: RANDOLPH Attorney General
for the United States.

The endorsement on the back reads:

Delivered to the within named Samuel Hopkins this fourth day of August 1790.

TH: JEFFERSON

The most active member of the Patent Board was Thomas Jefferson. Although he never took out any patents for himself, he was a student of science and a fertile inventor. A number of his devices may be seen at Monticello, his home in Charlottesville, Virginia. Jefferson's most practical invention was the correct form of the moldboard, a curved iron plate attached to a plowshare that lifts, turns, and pulverizes the soil. His revolving chair was called by his political enemies "Jefferson's whirligig." They said he had devised it "so as to look all ways at once."

The members of the Patent Board soon encountered the problem of "interference," which occurs when two or more applicants try to patent virtually the same invention, but even nonconflicting applications put a heavy burden on these three very important and busy officials. Jefferson commented that the patent applications required a great deal of time to understand and treat with justice—more time indeed than members of the board could spare from more important duties.

With Jefferson's assistance, Congress looked for a system that would not make such heavy demands on high officials. The result was the Patent Act of 1793, which eliminated the requirement that the invention be "sufficiently useful or important." Examination was dropped, and patents were merely registered. Under the looser Act of 1793, the Patent Office emerged as a distinct State Department bureau in 1802 and for a quarter-century was strongly influenced by a remarkable administrator.

THE EXTRAORDINARY DR. THORNTON

Dr. William Thornton, a shining ornament of Washington's intellectual and social life for thirty years, was the first chief of the Patent Office and by all odds the least inhibited. He saw nothing wrong in granting patents to himself—a practice now prohibited by law. In one case, after suggesting an improvement to an inventor, he became a joint patentee.

During his long term as chief, from 1802 until 1828, Dr. Thornton operated the Patent Office in a highly proprietary manner, keeping records or not as he liked, making arbitrary decisions about fees—and frequently complaining to the successive secretaries of State at the low pay and lack of clerical help. But he made up in enthusiasm for his disregard of the legal niceties and is credited with originating several valuable procedures. One was the reissuance without additional fee of a patent in which defects were discovered.

Dr. Thornton, as architect, author, inventor, painter, political economist, and administrator, practiced almost all the arts except the one for which he had been educated—medicine. He left his mark not only on the patent system but on the Washington skyline. His was the winning design for the United States Capitol, and the Octagon, a fine dwelling that he built in Washington, D.C., has been preserved by the American Institute of Architects as its headquarters.

This extraordinary man was born on the little island of Jost Van Dykes in the British Virgin Islands on May 20, 1759. In 1784 Aberdeen University granted him his medical degree. After two years in Paris and a brief period at Tortola, near his birthplace, he came to the United States in 1787. He adopted Philadelphia as his home and in 1788 became an American citizen. In Philadelphia Thornton became interested in the mechanic arts. John Fitch demonstrated his first steamboat operated with paddles on the Delaware River in 1787. The next year his second steamer, in which Thornton had an interest, made a trip of twenty miles. Fitch's third steamer, the *Thornton,* achieved a speed of eight miles an hour and is said to have covered several thousand miles in regular trips as a packet boat before it was retired in the winter of 1790.

Upon his marriage in 1790, Thornton returned to Tortola for a two-year stay. Here he learned of the competition for the design of public buildings in Washington and wrote the commissioners of the federal city that he was bringing plans.

Thornton drew a design for the Capitol that was warmly praised by President Washington and won from the commissioners the award of $500 and a plot of land in the new city worth about the same amount.

In 1794 Thornton was himself appointed a commissioner and moved to Washington from Philadelphia. As he was neither an experienced architect nor a builder, his designs for the national Capitol could not be followed exactly, but Thornton felt that he had a mandate to see that his plans were executed and attempted to enforce them. The north and south wings of the building show his influence, and his idea for a great central rotunda was followed by other architects.

Congress abolished the board of commissioners in May, 1802. A few months later, James Madison, Secretary of State, appointed Thornton "to have charge of the issuing of patents" in the State Department. Later he was given his title of Superintendent of Patents. Madison and Thornton were next-door neighbors in Georgetown, then on the outskirts of the capital city, and were joint owners of a race horse. The salary of the Superintendent was only $1,400 a year, subsequently increased to $1,500, but Dr. Thornton was a friend of Franklin, Jefferson, Washington, and John Randolph—and, particularly, of the Madisons—and managed somehow to finance the necessary entertaining.

His vigor and personality were such that, when in 1814 Dr. Thornton persuaded the British not to burn the Patent Office, it was easy for people to believe the report that he had thrown himself at the cannon mouths. Dr. Thornton's own account, given in a letter to the public a few days after the threatened fire, is much more modest. He had removed the office records to his farm the day before the British entered Washington, but the patent models, which accompanied most applications, were too many and too bulky to move. The Patent Office was then in Blodgett's Hotel, a far from fireproof brick building of two stories, with basement and attic, at the northeast corner of Eighth and E streets in northwest Washington. Dr. Thornton wrote:

> Hearing next morning, (August 25th), while at breakfast in Georgetown, that the British were preparing to burn the War office and the public building containing the models of the arts, I was desirous not only of saving a [musical] instrument that had cost me great labour, but of preserving, if possible, the building and all the models—I therefore left my breakfast and hastened forward. . . . I . . . called on Mr. Nicholson, my model maker and messenger and desired him to attend me, he did, and the British soldiers were then marching in two columns to burn the building. When we arrived there we found the Rev'd Mr. Brown, Mr. Lyon and Mr. Hatfield near the Patent Office. Major Waters, who was then on guard and waiting the command of Colonel Jones, informed me that the private property might be taken out, I told him that there was nothing but private property of any consequence and that any public property to which he objected might be burnt in the street, provided the building might be preserved, which contained hundreds of models of the arts, and that it would be impossible to remove them, and to burn what would be useful to all mankind, would be as barbarous as formerly to burn the Alexandrian Library for which the Turks have been ever since condemned by all the enlightened nations. The Major desired me to go again with him to Col. Jones, who was attending some of his men engaged in destroying Mr. Gale's types and printing apparatus. I went to the Avenue and was kindly received by the Colonel; they took their men away and promised to spare the building.

The Patent Office was the only federal building not burned by the British forces. While the Capitol was being restored, the building housed Congress for the entire session of September 19, 1814, to March 3, 1815.

Dr. Thornton's freehanded administration ended with his death, March 28, 1828. A memorandum in his papers listed eight patents issued in his own name between 1802 and

1827, dealing with improvements in boilers, stills, firearms, and other devices. Since his day, no one has directed the Patent Office for a period approaching the Thornton quarter-century. However, individuality in its administration did not die with Dr. Thornton. One of his successors, Dr. John D. Craig, appointed Superintendent on June 11, 1829, was a man of vigor and controversy. In 1831 he rendered the following typically negative report to the Secretary of State, Edward Livingston, on a candidate for a clerkship:

> The man about three years ago, married a young lady with a large fortune, and in a short time spent the whole of it in dissipation, with abandoned associates. I hope a public office will not, during the present administration, be the reward of such conduct.

Dr. Craig fought violently with patent applicants, including one William P. Elliot, who was later to design a new Patent Office building. Mr. Elliot charged the redoubtable Dr. Craig with, among other things, ignorance of the law, destruction of public correspondence, rude conduct in his official relations, and other malfeasance. After prolonged wrangling, Dr. Craig was convicted of categorizing an order by one of his superiors as "tyrannical and unjust." He was finally dismissed from office on January 31, 1835.

THE GREAT FIRE OF 1836

The British did not burn the Patent Office, but twenty-two years later someone else did—no doubt by accident. Its history for many years was affected by its quarters, sometimes cramped, sometimes elegant, and now and then destroyed along with records and the models of inventions.

In its infancy, the Patent Office lived with its parent, the State Department, at various temporary addresses. The records could be handled by one clerk and "did not fill over a dozen pigeon holes." Most of the first ten years were spent in Philadelphia, with the exception of a three-month period in Trenton, New Jersey, during a yellow fever epidemic. After the government moved from Philadelphia to Washington early in 1800, home for the Patent Office was at 1901 Pennsylvania Avenue Northwest, in a building that was not torn down until 1959. It was also housed in a structure at Seventeenth and G streets Northwest, on part of the site occupied by that vast pillared monument long called the Old State, War, and Navy Building, but now known officially as the Executive Office Building.

By 1810 the Patent Office, under Dr. Thornton's lively direction, needed separate quarters of its own, and the government bought Blodgett's Hotel at Eighth and E streets, which was long its home. At first, the Patent Office had four rooms on the second floor. In 1829 an addition was built at the Seventh Street end for the Patent Office and the City Post Office. With the growth of the country there was a corresponding growth in the number of patent models, and space was always a problem. On July 4, 1836, Congress authorized construction of a new building for the Patent Office. Less than six months later, on December 15, fire gutted Blodgett's Hotel, which Dr. Thornton had saved from the British torch. A messenger who slept on the premises discovered the fire about 3 A.M. Apparently it had started in the cellar, where fuel was stored, and had gained much headway. The flames licked through the tindery wooden floors and consumed all the records that the Patent Office possessed. By the time the "engines and buckets" arrived, it was too late for the firemen to save anything.

The loss was estimated at 7,000 models, 9,000 drawings, and 230 books, in addition to the applications, correspondence, and copies of issued patents. The next year Congress appropriated $100,000 to restore the records and to obtain replicas of the most important models. From court records, and with the assistance of inventors who held the original patents, a partial recovery was made.

A WIDE LOOPHOLE FOR FRAUD

During the early years of the Patent Office, a number of famous inventions were produced that had their effect on the American economy and American manners. These included the cotton gin (Eli Whitney, 1794), the reaper (Cyrus H. McCormick, 1834), and the six-shooter (Samuel Colt, 1836). But in addition to these, the registration system established in 1793 had encouraged a mass of worthless and conflicting patents and had flooded the courts with disputes. Some patents were issued for "inventions" long in public use. Senator John Ruggles, a freshman senator from Maine, led the fight for reform.

"For more than forty years," he reported to the Senate in 1836, "the Department of State has issued patents on every application, without any examination into the merits or novelty of the invention." There were scandalous goings on in the Patent Office itself. The 1793 law, he insisted,

opens the door to frauds, which have already become extensive and serious. It is represented to the committee that it is not uncommon for persons to copy patented machines in the model room; and, having made some light immaterial alterations, they apply in the next room for patents. There being no power to refuse them, patents are issued of course. Thus prepared, they go forth on a retailing expedition, selling out their patent rights for States, counties and townships, to those who have no means at hand of detecting the imposition, and who find, when it is too late, that they have purchased what the venders had no right to sell, and which they obtain thereby no right to use. This speculation in patent rights has become a regular business, and several hundred thousand dollars, it is estimated, are paid annually for void patents, many of which are thus fraudulently obtained.

The Act of July 4, 1836, laid the foundation of the modern patent system. It re-established "the American system," which included the requirement of an examination to determine the novelty and usefulness of an invention. The chief of the office was to have the title of Commissioner of Patents and to be appointed by the President with the approval of the Senate. His salary was fixed at $3,000 a year.

The Patent Office, established as a distinct and separate bureau—but still in the Department of State—had an organization that, in miniature, forecast that of the modern agency. The Commissioner was to appoint a chief clerk, an examiner of patents, a machinist, two clerks as draftsmen, an inferior clerk, and a messenger. An appropriation of $1,500 was voted for the purchase of a library of scientific works and periodicals. Appeals from the decisions of the examiner of patents were permitted. Employees of the Patent Office were forbidden to acquire any interest in a patent except by inheritance or bequest. An application fee of $30 was fixed by the 1836 law for citizens; aliens paid more. A patent was good for fourteen years subject to an extension of seven years upon approval of a special board consisting of the Secretary of State, the Solicitor of the Treasury, and the Commissioner of Patents. (The modern term is seventeen years.)

The numbering of patents began in 1836. And who received No. 1, which was issued July 13, 1836? It went to Senator John Ruggles, as inventor of a "Locomotive Steam-Engine for Rail and Other Roads . . . designed to give a multiplied tractive power to the locomotive and to prevent the evil of the sliding of the wheels."

Henry L. Ellsworth, Superintendent of Patents, became the first Commissioner under the 1836 law. He had been president of the Aetna Insurance Company. Commissioner Ellsworth helped Samuel F. B. Morse obtain a congressional appropriation of $30,000 to test the practicability of the telegraph. He also, innocently, created the report, still widely credited today, that sometime in the nineteenth century the head of the Patent Office resigned because everything had already been invented. In his annual report for 1843, Ellsworth indulged in a rhetorical flourish to emphasize the progress of invention in his day. It was this sentence that started the myth: "The advancement of the arts, from year to year, taxes our credulity and seems to presage the arrival of that period when human improvement must end."

The youngest man ever appointed Commissioner was William Darius Bishop. A former congressman, he was named seventh Commissioner of Patents by President James Buchanan in 1859. The vigorous young Commissioner (he was thirty-one) exhibited an independence of spirit even against his former colleagues. It had been the practice to issue lengthy annual reports on the work of the Patent Office, and Congress decreed a limit of 800 pages. Commissioner Bishop published one of 1,800 pages and got away with it. After his term he became president of the New York, New Haven, and Hartford Railroad.

A few years earlier, in 1855, Clara Barton, one of the first women to receive an appointment in the federal service, was employed in the Patent Office on a piece-work basis. Later she was employed full-time at $1,400 a year, which was near the top for a clerical salary. She left in 1857, but returned in 1860 and served until 1865. When the wounded were brought in from Antietam, she left her duties to care for them. After the war, she founded the American Red Cross.

In the postwar period, the office of Commissioner of Patents went to several deserving Union generals. Two of them gave recognition to the importance of women in the office: General Mortimer D. Leggett (1871-74) authorized the hiring of a "lady clerk" for each examining division and issued an order that qualified women be accepted for the post of third assistant examiner, and Herbert Eleazer Paine (1878-80) installed in his office the first typewriter used in the bureau and, against vigorous protests, put these time-saving machines into all divisions as fast as the typists could be hired.

Since the 1880's, almost without exception, the commissioners have been lawyers, most of whom had specialized in patent practice. A few came up through the Patent Office ranks but all had to meet political qualifications. The shortest term—about a month—was that of Melvin H. Coulston, appointed in the dying days of the Woodrow Wilson Administration and succeeded in 1921 by Thomas E. Robertson, a Harding appointee. The latter's term was the longest on record since the passage of the Act of 1836—twelve years and two months. Conway P. Coe ranked next with just under a dozen years; his tenure ended in 1945. Some commissioners, including Robert C. Watson and William E. Schuyler, Jr., have been active in the patent bar associations.

THE NEW PATENT OFFICE HOME

For four years after the burning of Blodgett's Hotel in 1836, while the new Patent Office Building was under construction, the stricken agency occupied space in the old City Hall on Judiciary Square in northwest Washington at the head of John Marshall Place. William Parker Elliot designed the new building while he was still less than thirty years of age. It was to be the pride of the Patent Office staff for ninety-two years, from its opening in 1840 until 1932, when new quarters were provided in the Department of Commerce Building.

The first section of this impressive structure, which many Washington residents still call the old Patent Office Building, extended 270 feet along F Street, with its center portico facing south down Eighth Street. The long flight of steps that led up to the first floor was cut down in 1934 to permit the widening of F Street, but otherwise the old building, made of sandstone from Aquia Creek, Virginia, looks pretty much as it must have looked a century ago. It is now occupied by the Smithsonian

Institution's National Collection of Fine Arts and National Portrait Gallery. In his plans for the original design, Elliot wrote:

> The building is to be two stories high, resting upon an elevated basement. The order of architecture adopted for the exterior is Grecian Doric. . . . The details are modeled after the celebrated Parthenon. . . . The principal front . . . on F Street is graced with a portico of sixteen columns, octa-style arrangement, the columns, and entablature, and pediment being of the size and proportion of the Parthenon, each column being 18 feet in circumference at the base.

Here Elliot provided space for a museum with an adequate display of patent models. Here troops were quartered during the Civil War, and here Walt Whitman visited the wounded. On the first floor were the offices of the Commissioner of Patents and a model room. The second floor was one huge room—the largest in the United States at that time. Lincoln's second inaugural ball was held in this room on March 6, 1865. The *Daily National Intelligencer* reported that, after a military band struck up "Hail to the Chief," President Lincoln passed down the center of the great hall, escorted by the Honorable Schuyler Colfax. Then came Mrs. Lincoln, "most elegantly dressed," escorted by Senator Charles Sumner. By 1870, other wings had been added, to fill the entire block. The total cost of the building was $3 million.

The second great fire in the history of the Patent Office was discovered at 11 A.M. on Monday, September 24, 1877, under the roof of the Ninth Street entrance. It seems to have originated either in a hothouse in that wing or in an adjoining loft that contained four years' accumulation of rejected models. There was some difficulty in reaching the loft, and water pressure was insufficient. In response to telegrams, Alexandria, Virginia, sent a fire engine and four more engines came from Baltimore by train. According to the official report, the roof and model rooms and their contents on the west and north sides (Ninth Street and G Street sides) were completely destroyed. About 87,000 models were lost. Property loss was about $1 million. The damaged wings were restored and reoccupied in 1881.

CHANGES IN THE PATENT LAW

The 1836 Act had set the patent system on a firm foundation, and there was no major revision until 1870. In the interim, however, Congress transferred the Patent Office from the State Department to the Department of the Interior upon the latter's creation in 1849 and made several changes in patents themselves. A new class—design patents—was added in 1842 with a term of seven years. In 1861 inventors were given a choice of three and a half, seven, or fourteen years, a choice that they may exercise today. In 1861 also the term of patents proper, usually called invention patents, was changed from fourteen years (with possible extension to twenty-one) to a fixed term of seventeen years—the figure hit upon as a compromise. In 1862 the creation of the Department of Agriculture relieved the Patent Office of a minor job, the collection of statistics on agriculture. For some years it had also collected meteorological data.

The codification of the patent laws in 1870 was inspired by the brilliant twelfth Commissioner of Patents, Samuel Sparks Fisher. Historians recount that, as a precocious child of two, he could read a primer. At four he was reading the Bible. After practicing law and serving in the Civil War as an Ohio National Guard colonel, Fisher was given charge of the Patent Office in April, 1869. He introduced competitive examinations to improve the quality of the examining corps and made a number of innovations. On his own initiative, he contracted for ten copies of each drawing in the Patent Office to be produced by the new art of lithography. The specifications and drawings of all patents thereafter granted were issued in printed form.

If something was beyond Fisher's authority, he sought the cooperation of Congress. This occurred when he got Congress to approve consolidating the twenty-five acts and parts of acts passed in the previous thirty-four years. For one thing, the new law of 1870 made it unnecessary to submit a model unless it was required by the Commissioner. This saved costs for the applicant and storage space for the Patent Office, but, as it turned out, for another decade models were often required. Procedure in the settlement of interferences and in appeals from Patent Office decisions was improved, and the Commissioner was authorized to issue rules and regulations, subject to approval by the Secretary of the Interior.

One provision of the 1870 law resulted two years later in the inauguration of the weekly *Official Gazette,* in which abstracts of current patents are published and which carries decisions of general interest. Also under the new law, copyright matters, which had been handled by the Patent Office since 1859, were transferred to the Library of Congress. An exception was made four years later as to copyrights for prints and labels, which were left with the Patent Office until 1939. Since then all copyright registration has been conducted by the Library of Congress.

One section of the 1870 law authorized the Patent Office to register trademarks, but it was declared unconstitutional in 1879. A second Trademark Act, adopted in 1881, covered those used in foreign trade and business with the Indian tribes but was of little importance because it did not cover interstate commerce. It was not until 1905 that a broad and valid trademark law was passed by Congress.

The United States became a member in 1887 of the Paris Convention of 1883, formally known as the Convention for the Protection of Industrial Property (meaning patents and trademarks), under which members give nationals of other members the same rights they give their own citizens. Other steps in international cooperation have followed.

In 1930, with approving nods from Luther Burbank and Thomas A. Edison, Congress authorized a new class of patents —on botanical plants. Such a grant is made for seventeen years to anyone "who has invented or discovered and asexually reproduced any distinct and new variety of plant other than a tuber-propagated plant." Since then the chief work of the Patent Office has been, and still is, the granting of patents on inventions, designs, and plants and the registration of trademarks.

In 1940 the approach of World War II brought an act authorizing the Commissioner to keep defense inventions secret. Six years later the first Atomic Energy Act (revised 1954) prohibited the patenting of atomic weapons. Congress authorized in 1950 the extension of patents to World War II veterans who applied.

The second act since 1836 to completely rewrite and codify U.S. patent laws was signed by President Harry S Truman on July 19, 1952. It embodied many changes in arrangement and language intended to make it easier to understand, omitted obsolete sections, and incorporated interpretations by the courts. Extracts from the act (United States Code Title 35— Patents), as later amended, are given in Appendix B.

Separate but related laws are the National Aeronautics and Space Act of 1958, which governs the space agency's patent operations, and the Federal Food, Drug, and Cosmetic Act of 1962, which authorizes the Secretary of Health, Education, and Welfare to furnish the Patent Office answers to questions about drugs involved in patent applications.

From Commerce Building to Crystal Plaza

By executive order, the Patent Office was transferred in 1925 from the Department of the Interior to the Department of Commerce, of which it remains a part today. Four years later President Herbert Hoover laid the cornerstone of the Department of Commerce Building, using a trowel and gavel with which President Washington had laid the cornerstone of the Capitol on September 18, 1793. The new Commerce Building was to be a massive stone structure of seven stories, covering nearly eight acres, and forming the base of the so-called Federal Triangle of government buildings that now runs from Fifteenth Street to the juncture of Pennsylvania and Constitution Avenues. The contractors were surprised to find that ancient Tiber Creek, after being buried for nearly a century, was still flowing lustily under the site. They used its cool waters to air-condition the offices of the Secretary of Commerce on the fifth floor. Into this building the Patent Office moved in 1932.

Across the north, or E Street, end was the Public Search Room, where lawyers, professional searchers, and inventors shuffled "hard" (cardboard) copies of U.S. patents to find out whether ideas were new or had been patented before. For the Commissioner and many divisions, including the examining staff, the Commerce Building was to be home for 35 years—except for a temporary removal to Richmond during World War II. As the agency grew, supplemental space was rented in other buildings. At this writing, the only sections of the Patent Office still in the Commerce Building are Patent Copy Sales and a reproduction unit. In two and a half acres of basement are stored more than 100 million printed copies of patents. As conditions change, and photocopying becomes more general, what remains there of the Patent Office will probably be moved to Crystal Plaza, across the Potomac.

A management survey conducted in 1961 and 1962 by Earl W. Kintner, a Washington lawyer, concluded that a new building was the only solution for the "chronic inadequacy of space and facilities." After exploring various sites, the agency moved in 1967 and 1968 to Crystal Plaza, a commercial and residential development near Washington in Arlington County, Virginia, off Jefferson Davis Highway. Here the Patent Office has leased three new eleven-story buildings and a two-story annex that joins two of them.

The shirt-sleeve charm of the dusty Commerce Building has been succeeded by a sophisticated and professional atmosphere better suited to the state of technology in the late twentieth century. Instead of looking out on the Ellipse near the White House, examiners who are fortunate in their desk assignments now have a view of an apartment house swimming pool on one side or, on the other side, the Potomac River and the National Airport, with the Capitol in the distance. The two-story structure houses the Search Center, with its millions of copies of U.S. and foreign patents and technical publications. In the new Public Search Room on the ground floor there are high windows, bright ceiling lights, a carpeted floor, long desks, and seats for 325.

In 180 years the Patent Office job has grown enormously, both in volume and complexity. Since Senator Ruggles got Patent No. 1 in 1836, more than 3.5 million patents have been granted for inventions, in addition to limited numbers on designs and plants. The number of modern invention patents —currently about 60,000 a year in response to about 90,000 applications—does not reflect the amount of work, for technology has become more and more complex. It is said that examiners can grant today only a fraction of the volume of patents that the same sized staff could have issued thirty years ago.

As a business organization, the Patent Office has been plagued by heavy backlogs of work, by the time lag between application and patent, by the turnover of personnel, by the difficulty of applying standards to anything as vague as invention, and by pressures for patent quality that will survive in court. The accomplishments and limitations are summarized elsewhere, but it is worth noting here that until about thirty-five years ago the agency made a profit for the government after supporting itself on fees.

This little agency, which still has fewer than 3,000 employees, has had its periods of low morale, but it has survived the years with a minimum of internal controversy. In modern times, there has been no scandal over the theft of an idea or even the disclosure of a pending application. Relationships with industry, inventors, and people in general have been chiefly through patent attorneys. The bar associations have kept an eye on the agency's operations.

There have been *external* controversies, however, as we shall see in Chapters IV and X. The patent monopoly has been studied by government commissions in the light of the antitrust laws and the concentration of wealth. Compulsory licensing has been recommended by the Temporary National Economic Committee and has been considered at various times by congressional committees, but has never been enacted as a general requirement.

A patent centennial celebration was held at Washington in April, 1891, with Alexander Graham Bell in attendance. Senator O. H. Platt of Connecticut, one of the speakers, remarked that American inventions dwarfed the pyramids. "Let me enumerate the seven wonders of American invention," he said. "The cotton-gin; the adaptation of steam to methods of transportation; the application of electricity in business pursuits; the harvester; the modern printing press; the ocean cable, and the sewing machine."

Dr. Samuel P. Langley, secretary of the Smithsonian Institution, looked into the possible inventions of the coming decade. "It would be rash to predict what these all may be," he said, "but I desire to express my personal conviction that one at least, which has been a mere dream of enthusiasts in the past, is soon to become a reality, and to venture the statement

that the air may probably be made to support engine-driven
flying machines, heavier than the air itself, before the expira-
tion of the present century."

The first successful experiment with a model plane was
Langley's own and was conducted on the Potomac River in
1896. Wilbur and Orville Wright made the first flight in an
airplane with an engine in 1903 and got their patent three
years later.

Since 1790 both the Patent Office and the country have
passed through the ages of steam, electricity, and chemistry,
into the age of electronics, which may as well be called the
age of the computer, space travel, and the split atom. The
American patent system has been a major factor in this country's advance to technological and commercial leadership of
the world. And the Patent Office has been at the center of the
administrative, judicial, industrial, and professional forces that
have made the system work.

II

The Patent Office Organization

The U.S. Department of Commerce, the parent agency of the Patent Office, is something of a conglomerate. Its functions include counting noses (Bureau of the Census), watching the weather (Environmental Science Services Administration*), promoting shipping (Maritime Administration), regulating measurement (National Bureau of Standards), and serving the businessman in many ways. In the departmental family, the most helpful sibling has been the National Bureau of Standards, which has assisted the Patent Office in the greater use of electronics in its work. Since 1812 there have been several official recommendations that the Patent Office be made an independent agency (the subject is treated in detail in Chapter X), but it is still very much a part of the Department of Commerce. In the departmental table of organization it comes under the jurisdiction of the assistant secretary of Commerce for Science and Technology.

The Commissioner of Patents, the immediate head of the agency, three of his assistants, and the examiners-in-chief are all appointed by the President, subject to Senate approval. The patent law (U.S. Code, Title 35, Section 3) provides that the Secretary of Commerce, "upon the nomination of the Com-

---

* As of December, 1970, the National Oceanic and Atmospheric Administration.

25

missioner . . . shall appoint all other officers and employees."
The statute provides further that "the Secretary of Commerce
may vest in himself the functions of the Patent Office and its
officers and employees specified in this [Act] and may from
time to time authorize their performance by any other officer
or employee."

The Commissioner is a sort of operations manager in the
Patent Office. The Act covers his duties in these words:

> The Commissioner, under the direction of the Secretary of Com-
> merce, shall superintend or perform all duties required by law
> respecting the granting and issuing of patents and the registra-
> tion of trademarks; and he shall have charge of property belong-
> ing to the Patent Office. He may, subject to the approval of the
> Secretary of Commerce, establish regulations, not inconsistent
> with law, for the conduct of proceedings in the Patent Office.

The Organization Today

Dr. Myron Tribus, dean of the Thayer School of Engineering at Dartmouth College, was appointed assistant secretary of
Commerce for Science and Technology in March, 1969. Also
nominated by President Richard M. Nixon was William E.
Schuyler, Jr., who took office as Commissioner of Patents in
May. By custom and tradition, commissioners had long been
patent lawyers, and Mr. Schuyler was no exception. He had
practiced in that field since 1940 and had been chairman of
the Patent, Trademark, and Copyright Law Section of the
American Bar Association. Mr. Schuyler succeeded Edward J.
Brenner, who had served for more than five years. At the time
of his appointment in 1964, Mr. Brenner was assistant director
of the Legal Division of Esso Research and Engineering Company. He had served as an enlisted man in the army in World
War II and had been a member of the radiological safety team
at the Bikini atom bomb tests.

CHART I Organization Chart of the Patent Office

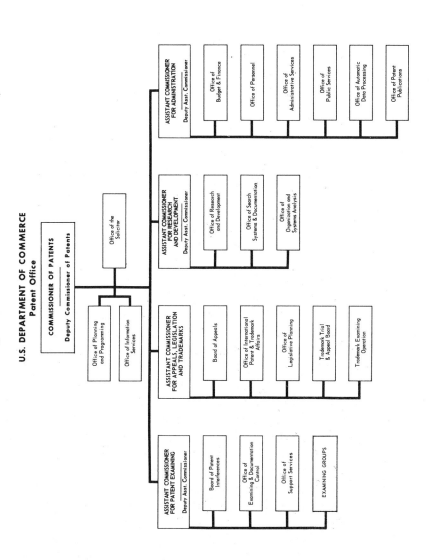

U.S. DEPARTMENT OF COMMERCE
Patent Office

COMMISSIONER OF PATENTS
Deputy Commissioner of Patents

Office of the Solicitor

Office of Planning and Programming

Office of Information Services

ASSISTANT COMMISSIONER FOR PATENT EXAMINING
Deputy Asst. Commissioner

- Board of Patent Interferences
- Office of Examining & Documentation Control
- Office of Support Services
- EXAMINING GROUPS

ASSISTANT COMMISSIONER FOR APPEALS, LEGISLATION AND TRADEMARKS
Deputy Asst. Commissioner

- Board of Appeals
- Office of International Patent & Trademark Affairs
- Office of Legislative Planning
- Trademark Trial & Appeal Board
- Trademark Examining Operation

ASSISTANT COMMISSIONER FOR RESEARCH AND DEVELOPMENT
Deputy Asst. Commissioner

- Office of Research and Development
- Office of Search Systems & Documentation
- Office of Organization and Systems Analysis

ASSISTANT COMMISSIONER FOR ADMINISTRATION
Deputy Asst. Commissioner

- Office of Budget & Finance
- Office of Personnel
- Office of Administrative Services
- Office of Public Services
- Office of Automatic Data Processing
- Office of Patent Publications

Six months after Mr. Schuyler took office he announced a reorganization, which he had worked out with the Department of Commerce (see Chart I). Fresh from his law practice, he was aware of the patent bar's criticisms of Patent Office delays. In an interview he explained that the changes were designed to expedite the handling of patent applications and to render more efficient service to the public. The principal organizational changes were the addition of two assistant commissioners—one for research and development and the other for administration—and the creation of a unit called the Office of Public Services. For the first time there was to be a deputy commissioner of Patents (previously the senior aide had been known as first assistant commissioner).

As shown in the accompanying chart, three offices report directly to the Commissioner (Office of Planning and Programming, Office of Information Services, and Office of the Solicitor).

The Office of Planning and Programming develops plans based on the goals and objectives that the Commissioner designates and analyzes alternative ways of reaching them from the standpoint of cost-effectiveness. The Office of Information Services handles press and other relations with the public, as described in Chapter IX.

The Office of the Solicitor consists of the chief legal officer and his assistants. They handle all legal matters to which the Commissioner is a party and represent him in certain courts (see Chapter VII). The solicitor also drafts legislation, in cooperation with the Office of Legislative Planning, which maintains direct contacts with congressional committees.

Internal disputes are passed on by three boards. The Board of Appeals decides on appeals from adverse decisions of examiners rejecting claims in patent applications. The Board of Patent Interferences rules on disputes between rival inventors over the priority of invention. The Trademark Trial and Appeal Board handles oppositions, cancellations, interferences, appeals from examiners' decisions, and related matters. The titles of the four assistant commissioners, and the units reporting to them are:

Assistant Commissioner for Patent Examining: Board of Patent Interferences, Office of Examining and Documentation Control, Office of Support Services, and the fifteen examining groups.

Assistant Commissioner for Appeals, Legislation, and Trademarks: Board of Appeals, Office of International Patent and Trademark Affairs, Office of Legislative Planning, Trademark Trial and Appeal Board, and Trademark Examining Operation.

Assistant Commissioner for Research and Development: Office of Research and Development, Office of Search Systems and Documentation, and Office of Organization and Systems Analysis.

Assistant Commissioner for Administration: Office of Administrative Services, Office of Public Services, Office of Automatic Data Processing, and Office of Patent Publications.

The deputy commissioner and two assistant commissioners are Presidential appointees. The Secretary of Commerce has authority to name the other two assistant commissioners. The assistant commissioners get about $30,000 a year. (In 1969 Congress increased the salary of the Commissioner to $36,000.)

The Office of Public Services is in charge of the Search Center at Crystal Plaza in Arlington County, Virginia, where an inventor may go to find out for himself whether his concept has already been patented. Besides maintaining the collections of U.S. and foreign patents and technical literature for the use of the patent and trademark examiners and the public, the unit's duties include furnishing copies of patents and office records, recording assignments of patents and trademarks, and providing drafting services. Much of the work is done on a fee basis.

As its name implies, the Office of International Patent and Trademark Affairs maintains relations with foreign patent offices on treaties and on cooperative activities in searching, classification, and training. Some of the other units require a few words of explanation:

The Office of Examining and Documentation Control checks the quality of the examining and classification work. The Office of Support Services provides clerical help to the examiners and handles applications before and after they are examined.

The Office of Research and Development devises computer and other mechanical search and retrieval equipment and procedures (see Chapter III). The Office of Search Systems and Documentation develops the classes and subclasses used. The Office of Organization and Systems Analysis works out methods and procedures for the entire Patent Office. The Office of Automatic Data Processing maintains and operates computers and prepares computer programs, providing services to other Patent Office units.

The Staff and Its Tasks

How big is the staff, and what does it do? As federal agencies go, the Patent Office is small, but its educational level is high. The number of employees has been relatively stable for five years—about 2,600 in fiscal 1969. More than half were listed as professionals—holders of one or more college degrees—and most of these were patent examiners.

The examining corps (1,177 in fiscal 1969) constitutes the largest group of Patent Office employees and has the most interesting and important job. Its members pass on applications for patents and deal by mail, telephone, and sometimes office conferences with attorneys and inventors. After studying an application and doing the necessary research, an examiner recommends that a patent be allowed if it meets the tests of novelty, utility, and invention. If it does not, he rejects the claims, and the applicant or his attorney tries to amend the claims so that they pass the requirements. The duties of an examiner are discussed in more detail in Appendix A (Career Opportunities).

Examiners have their own files of patents relating to their special fields of interest. Patent copies are kept in drawers (referred to as "shoe boxes") that pull out from the wall. Copies of some patents have been microfilmed on so-called aperture cards and may be read in desk viewers. The aperture card method of searching, which is described in the next chapter, is expected eventually to become general. Future examiners will be able to rely increasingly on computer aid.

Fifteen groups of examiners pass on applications and grant patents in these categories:

General Chemistry and Petroleum Chemistry
General Organic Chemistry
High Polymer Chemistry, Plastics and Molding
Coating and Laminating, Bleaching, Dyeing, and Photography
Specialized Chemical Industries and Chemical Engineering
Industrial Electronics and Related Elements
Security and Designs
Information Transmission, Storage, and Retrieval
Electronic Component Systems and Devices
Physics
Handling and Transportation Media
Material Shaping, Article Manufacturing, Tools
Amusement, Husbandry, Personal Treatment, Information
Heat and Power Engineering
Constructions, Supports, Textiles, Cleaning

Related units train new examiners, classify and reclassify patents, provide clerical support for the examining groups, and maintain the files consulted in searching the prior art.

The Trademark Examining Operation, which classifies, examines, and registers trademarks and service marks, does its important job with a relatively small staff. The number of employees in fiscal 1969 was 106, of whom 54 were trademark examiners or attorneys, all with college degrees. Vacancies in the examining staff are usually filled with law school graduates. Public files of registered marks and indexes of pending applications may be examined in a trademark search room at the Crystal Plaza offices. Access to a pending trademark file may be had upon a written showing of good cause (the files on pending patents are kept secret). Additional information on examiners and their duties will be found in Appendix A.

One Patent Office problem has been a high turnover, particularly among the examiners. In 1964 Dr. J. Herbert Hollomon, Assistant Secretary of Commerce for Science and Technology, called the Patent Office the primary source for the education, training, and internship of the American patent bar. "The average tenure of a patent examiner," he told a lawyers' meeting, "is five and a half years, and it is estimated that it takes three of that five and a half years to become expert enough to contribute significantly to the examination and searching process. That means that the lifetime of an examiner in the Patent Office is really only two and a half years, and he is hardly then beginning to reach the peak of his examination effectiveness." The turnover was at that time, and for some years had been, about 20 per cent annually. By early 1969 it had been reduced to 12 per cent. The lowered resignation rate and generally improved morale have been attributed to several factors:

1. Higher salaries prevailing in federal agencies, making the jobs more competitive with those in industry
2. Greatly improved quarters in the modern buildings in Crystal Plaza, Arlington County, Virginia, to which the examiners and most of the Patent Office staff moved in 1967 and 1968

3. Payment by the Patent Office of about three-quarters of the cost of night law-school courses, to be refunded by any examiner who leaves within five years

4. Earlier delegation of authority to sign actions on patent applications, with less emphasis on seniority

In the period since World War II, the number of examining divisions has been reduced from seventy to fifteen groups. The chief examiners of the seventy groups made all the decisions for cases referred to their groups. During Mr. Ladd's and Mr. Brenner's tenures (1961–69) the total number of groups was reduced to thirty-one and then sixteen, while increased responsibility was delegated to examiners below the rank of division chief. Mr. Schuyler, the present Commissioner, has cut the number of divisions to fifteen. As of mid-1970 about 440 examiners, including 100 supervisory examiners, had full authority to sign actions.

SURVEYS AND CHANGES

Periodically since 1890 the Patent Office has been examined and investigated by congressional committees, private organizations hired for the purpose, and segments of the executive branch of government. Several surveys were conducted in the mid-1940's.

As World War II was coming to an end and the bulk of the Patent Office was still in Richmond, the Bureau of the Budget studied the agency's setup and was not pleased with what it found. A memorandum dated July 3, 1945, addressed to a Department of Commerce official, pointed out that twenty-eight officials reported directly to the Commissioner, that there was nothing in the way of a planning or administrative staff, and that too much was required of the chief clerk, who had charge of ten clerical divisions. Among the changes urged were improved intermediate supervision of the professional and clerical operations, the strengthening of budget and personnel services, and better management of reproduction and patent copy sales. "A less immediate but highly important step," stated the report, "is a study of the organization of the examining corps, now divided into 65 examining divisions."

Improvements were demanded in the classification system (see Chapter III), in the status of examiners, and in their procedures. The Bureau of the Budget objected to the six months allowed applicants to respond to office actions (rejections of claims) and to pay the final fee. The law has since been amended to require payment of the final fee within three months. The Commissioner already had authority to set a shorter period for office actions; in practice, this is usually three months also.

Under Casper W. Ooms, who succeeded Conway P. Coe as Commissioner in July, 1945, the administrative and service functions were reorganized. One official recalls the principal changes as appointment of "a few more chiefs." The chief clerk, it may be noted, was shifted.

The Department of Commerce annual report for 1947 recorded that "as reorganized, the Patent Office comprises the Office of the Commissioner of Patents, which includes the Board of Appeals and the Office of the Solicitor, and three major operating components. These are the Patent Examining Operation, the Trademark Examining Operation, and the Executive Office. Each is assigned a major function of the Patent Office activities under the direction of a single administrator who reports to, and is responsible to, the Commissioner."

President Truman had on April 20, 1945, asked Henry A. Wallace, Secretary of Commerce, to appoint a Department of Commerce Patent Survey Committee. William H. Davis, Director of Economic Stabilization, was appointed chairman; the other members were Tom C. Clark, Attorney General; Dr. Vannevar Bush, director of the Office of Scientific Research and Development; and Charles F. Kettering, chairman of the National Patent Planning Commission. Mr. Truman wanted recommendations on legislative proposals to lay before Congress, but no report was ever published.

Wallace Clark and Company, a New York firm of management consultants, concluded for the Patent Office in 1948 a survey of the examining operation and made recommendations for gradual reduction of the backlog of pending cases.

Among the Patent Office problems cited in a 1962 management survey conducted by Robert C. Kintner, a Washington lawyer and former chairman of the Federal Trade Commission, were high turnover, the need for new quarters, undue emphasis on seniority in promotion, and the general lack of a sense of urgency. These appear to have been eliminated or improved, but there is no easy cure for one other problem: the geometrical expansion of technology.

Mr. Kintner appended to his report a complaint by twenty-five Negroes employed in the Commerce Building basement who charged that they were discriminated against and that rats, bats, squirrels, and insects inhabited the files of printed patents among which they worked. The patent copies, they said, were infested with paper lice and, when the papers were pulled out, dust and debris fell into the workers' faces. As a result of the management survey, sanitation and morale improved,* but it was difficult to keep several acres of basement entirely free of contamination—and still more difficult to keep paper lice out of a hundred million documents, some of them a century old. At the direction of David L. Ladd, then Commissioner of Patents, ventilation was improved, and employees were cautioned not to leave lunch scraps around for rodents. Officials who investigated the complaints found

---

* The Patent Office had been high in the number of complaints of racial discrimination, but by 1969—when approximately 38 per cent of Patent Office employees were Negroes—the number of such complaints had dropped to zero. On June 29, 1970, Lutrelle F. Parker, the first Negro to be named an examiner-in-chief and member of the Patent Office Board of Appeals, was sworn in by Secretary of Commerce Maurice H. Stans. Mr. Parker had joined the Patent Office as a patent examiner in 1948.

one bat but no basement squirrels. However, Mr. Ladd's predecessors had occupied a ground-floor suite, with windows opening on a tree-lined parking strip, and reporters recalled meeting a squirrel now and then in those quarters, but it was usually sitting on a window sill, scratching and eating nuts proffered by the staff.

Over the years, the Patent Office has evolved, but there have been no radical reforms. The number and assignments of assistant commissioners have changed. Examining divisions have been altered in number, size, and province. The emphasis has shifted from mechanical to chemical and electronic inventions. Among the new units recently added to the agency have been the Office of Information Services, the Office of Research and Development, and the Trademark Trial and Appeal Board, all during the administration of Commissioner Watson in the Eisenhower years; the Patent Office Academy, under Commissioner Ladd (1961–63); and the Office of International Patent and Trademark Affairs, under Commissioner Brenner (1964–69).

Administrative histories, like tables of organization, make dull reading. Actually the Patent Office is a very human institution, made up of men and women who have chosen government as a career and are anxious to serve their employers— and their employers are the American people in general and inventors and patent owners in particular.

III

How the Patent Office Does Its Job

Through the Patent Office, America gives inventors a chance to profit by their ingenuity. The agency has kept pace with its task pretty well, despite a work load that over the years has grown enormously both in volume and in technical complexity. Since 1790, more than 3.5 million patents have been granted. The inventors remain uncounted, for many have received a dozen or a hundred apiece. (Thomas A. Edison held 1,093.) Some of the inventors have made fortunes for themselves or their employers. Others have gained little but a sense of recognition, and some have been merely out of pocket.

Most of the 3.5 million patents are now in the public domain, as their terms have expired. The monetary value of the more than 800,000 still in effect cannot be calculated. Corporations often carry them in their balance sheets at nominal amounts. Some clue may be found in the fact that, according to the National Science Foundation, industry was spending nearly $9 billion and government almost $15 billion in calendar 1969 for research and development, and both industry and government expected to get their money's worth in patents or know-how.

In our modern economy, invention has become largely an industrial activity. About three out of four patents today are issued to corporations, assigned by engineers, chemists, and physicists in accordance with their employment contracts. Studies by the PTC (Patent, Trademark, and Copyright) Research Institute of George Washington University indicate that about half of all patented inventions are used at some time before they expire. In this respect the employed inventors score a little better than the independents, but the field is entirely open to anyone who can pay the attorneys' and Patent Office fees. Farmers, housewives, Russians, and little girls get American patents, although it must be admitted that tot inventors usually have fathers who are patent lawyers.

What does the instrument confer? A United States patent gives its owner the right to exclude others from making, using, or selling the protected invention in this country for seventeen years from the date of issuance. As it is awarded only after a careful examination, the grant carries an assumption of validity, but it may be upset in court. And the "excluding" has to be done by the inventor or other owner, because the government does not go into court to do it for him.

Patents are a legacy from the Founding Fathers. Among the powers bestowed on the Congress by the Constitution—besides punishing piracies and felonies committed on the high seas, declaring war, and granting letters of marque and reprisal—was authority "To promote the Progress of Science and useful Arts, by securing for limited Times to Authors and Inventors the exclusive Right to their respective Writings and Discoveries." The present patent law, extracts from which are given in Appendix B, provides that "whoever invents or discovers any new and useful process, machine, manufacture, or composition of matter, or any new and useful improvement thereof, may obtain a patent therefor." One condition is that the invention must not be obvious to an artisan with ordinary skill.

MEASURES OF EFFICIENCY

How successful has the Patent Office been in carrying out the duties imposed by the Constitution and Congress? Its success may be judged by its speed in processing the applications it receives, by the volume of applications it disposes of (either by allowances or final rejections), by the complexity of the inventions patented, and by the soundness of the patents it issues—that is, by how well they hold up in court, if challenged. An additional criterion might be: How well does the Patent Office take advantage of modern technology in its own work?

It still takes an average of about two and a half years from filing to issuance of a patent, if one is allowed. In the case of electronic circuits and other involved inventions, the period may run to four or five years. Interference disputes (disputes between rival inventors, each claiming to be first) often end up in court and prolong the delay. A few of the patents issued in an average week are ten years old. Some, of course, go through in a few months.

The longest pending period was thirty-six years and nine days for Patent 1,203,190, received by the heirs of Charles Edgar Fritts on October 31, 1916. Fritts had filed his application for Recording and Reproduction of Pulsations in Sounds and Other Phenomena on October 22, 1880. The second longest wait, more than twenty-six years, was endured by William S. Gubelmann of Rochester, New York, who filed a patent application for his Calculating Machine on July 2, 1889, and got Patent 1,160,071 on November 9, 1915.

Recently there have been delays of more than twenty years. General Motors Corporation received on April 5, 1955, an important patent on the automatic choke, for which Peter J. Jorgensen and his son, Clarence H., had filed on January 8, 1932. Peter Jorgensen died the year after the application was filed. General Motors, which bought the invention, carried four adverse Patent Office decisions to the U.S. District Courts and won on most counts. By the time Patent 2,705,484 was granted, its principles had been embodied in many thousands of American automobiles, and General Motors could enforce its rights for another seventeen years. After interference actions lasting nearly a score of years, the Chrysler Corporation received on December 15, 1950, fifteen patents on inventions involving automatic power transmission. Some of the applications, including one signed by Carl A. Neracher, had been filed in 1939, and others in 1940 and 1941. Many of the features in the patents were still basic to automatic shifts. The interferences were so long drawn out and complex that an examiner-expert in the Patent Office received an award of $300 and a citation for his work on them. Several were carried to the Court of Customs and Patent Appeals. In other cases, long delays have occurred because the inventions were considered vital to national defense and were held in secrecy for years.

Besides disputes and the heavy backlog of applications (discussed below), the causes of delay include shortages of trained examiners and limited appropriations. An examiner takes his first action on a new application when he gets to it in the order of its filing date. The law provides that the response from the inventor or his attorney must be made within six months and gives the Commissioner authority to fix a shorter period, not under thirty days. In practice, this is usually set in each case at ninety days, and the examiner tries to act on the response within sixty days. Often inventors and their employers are in no hurry to have a patent granted, because the later it is issued the later it will expire. To correct this lag on the part of the public, an amendment of the patent law has often been proposed that would fix the term of a patent at twenty years from the filing date instead of seventeen years from issuance.

Administrative steps taken by the Patent Office to expedite action have included efforts to enlarge and stabilize the examining force, so that trained men will be retained and the same examiner can handle a given case to conclusion. In what has been called the "streamlined examining program" or "compact prosecution," begun in 1962 and later intensified, the aim has been to make the examiner's first action more thorough and complete and to make his second action either allowance or final rejection.

In reply to complaints at delays, the Patent Office points out that the present 2.5-year average pendency from filing to issuance matches the lowest average in more than twenty years. One letter, replying to such a complaint added, "It should be noted that the continuing high filing rate of applications, the increasing mass of technology to be searched, the loss of trained examiners to industry and other private endeavor, as fast as eligible technical personnel could be recruited, and other factors, have prevented any substantial inroad on the total inventory of patent applications . . . which exceeded 200,000 shortly after and since World War II."

In recent years the annual output of patents has been between 60,000 and 70,000, as compared with 12,931 in 1869. And certainly modern technology—with the transistor, the laser, nuclear fission, and space rocketry—presents much greater difficulties in searching and examining than did the chiefly mechanical inventions of a century ago. A chart displayed at a meeting of Patent Office employees in 1962 showed that in the thirty years since 1932 the average annual number of disposals—allowances or final rejections—per examiner assistant had dropped from 160 to 80. Complexity had cut the output in half.

The growth of international trade has presented problems in getting protection for the same invention in many countries. The Patent Office has been at pains to coordinate its procedures with those abroad, so as to reduce for American and foreign inventors the duplication in work caused by varying laws and regulations.

Some 90,000 applications are filed each year, and patents are granted on roughly seven out of ten. The figures for the five fiscal years ending June 30, 1969, for "invention" patents (this excludes designs and plant patents) are given in Table I.

TABLE I

APPLICATIONS FILED, PATENTS GRANTED, AND PATENTS PENDING,
FISCAL YEARS 1965–69

Fiscal Year	Applications Filed	Patents Granted	Patents Pending
1965	88,908	52,914	206,922
1966	93,022	66,243	209,254
1967	88,167	70,028	200,739
1968	90,252	61,599	189,909
1969	96,342	61,957	184,660

Roughly a fifth of these patents went to residents of foreign countries. The number of patents granted in 1968 and 1969 was restricted by budget limitations on printing expenditures. Only 1,300 could be issued each week, but the examining staff was approving a good many more. As a result, a new kind of backlog, consisting of approved but unissued patents, was built up, amounting to 15,905 by the end of fiscal 1969.

In fiscal 1968, the Patent Office succeeded in cutting its familiar backlog of applications in the pre-examination and examination stages to less than 200,000 for the first time since 1962. The speedup had been achieved by four years of a streamlined examining program, in which more applications were disposed of than were filed. Roughly 100,000 went through while 90,000 new ones were coming in.

The total numbers of patents pending for fiscal years 1965-69 are given in Table I. The pending backlog figures include applications in preliminary stages, but more than half of these were ready for the examiners.

Relatively few patents get into court, but those that do have a high mortality rate. A study of the question, published in

The Encyclopedia of Patent Practice and Invention Management, discloses that, of 734 patents adjudicated in all the United States Circuit Courts of Appeals in the eleven years 1953–63, 57.4 per cent were held to be invalid. About three out of four invalidations were for lack of invention.

For an earlier but overlapping period, 1948–54, a report prepared for the Senate Judiciary Subcommittee on Patents, Trademarks, and Copyrights found that 62.7 per cent of the 429 patents involved were held invalid by the Courts of Appeals. The subcommittee report also showed that the United States Supreme Court considered 93 patents in the years 1925 through 1951 and held 57 of them to be invalid. Senator John L. McClellan, chairman of the subcommittee, remarked in 1969 that he had been rather appalled to learn that every one of the sixteen patents litigated during the previous two years in the Court of Appeals for the Eighth Circuit, which included his home state of Arkansas, had been declared invalid.

A compilation made by Richard A. Gausewitz, a California lawyer, and published in the *Journal of the Patent Office Society* for May, 1969, showed that of 179 patents adjudicated by the Courts of Appeals in all circuits between February 21, 1966, and December 1, 1968, 72.1 per cent were held invalid. Mr. Gausewitz asserted that the great majority of the federal judicial circuits had interpreted the Supreme Court's decision in *Graham* v. *Deere,* issued on the earlier date, as a mandate to invalidate a much larger percentage of patents. In the decision, the court approved the statutory standard of invention incorporated in the 1952 law and said it intended to maintain the high standard it had established over many years.

The invalidation percentages cannot be interpreted to mean that the hundreds of thousands of patents in effect during the same years were equally vulnerable. For one thing, probably only relatively weak patents are likely to be attacked in court. But the Patent Office wants to issue as sound patents as pos-

CHART II U.S. Patent Office Classification—1838

Class 1 —AGRICULTURE, INCLUDING INSTRUMENTS AND OPERATIONS

Class 2 —ARTS POLITE, FINE, AND ORNAMENTAL
   Including music, painting, sculpture, engraving, books, paper, printing, binding, jewelry, &c.

Class 3 —CALORIFIC
   Comprising lamps, fire-places, stoves, grates, room-heaters, cooking apparatus, fuel, &c.

Class 4 —CHEMICAL MANUFACTURES, PROCESSES AND COMPOUNDS
   Including medicine, dyeing, color-making, distilling, mortars, cements, &c.

Class 5 —CIVIL ENGINEERING
   Comprising works on rail and common roads, bridges, canals, wharves, docks, rivers, weirs, dams, and other internal improvements

Class 6 —FIBROUS AND TEXTILE SUBSTANCES
   Including machines for preparing and manufacturing the fibres of wool, cotton, silk, fur, &c.

Class 7 —FIRE-ARMS AND IMPLEMENTS OF WAR, AND PARTS THEREOF
   Including manufacture of shot and gunpowder

Class 8 —GRINDING MILLS AND MILL-GEARING
   Containing grain mills, mechanical movements, horse-power, &c.

Class 9 —HYDRAULICS AND PNEUMATICS
   Including water-wheels, wind-mills, and other implements operated by air or water, or employed in the raising and delivery of fluids

Class 10—HOUSEHOLD FURNITURE
   Including domestic implements, washing machines, soap and candle making, bread and cracker machines, feather dressing, &c.

Class 11—LAND CONVEYANCE
   Comprising carriages, cars, and other vehicles, used on roads, and parts thereof

Class 12—LEATHER
   Including tanning and dressing, manufacture of boots, shoes, saddlery, harness, &c.

Class 13—LEVER AND SCREW POWER
   Including presses for packing, expressing balances, windlasses, cranes, jacks, and other mechanical contrivances for raising weight, &c.

Class 14—MATHEMATICAL, PHILOSOPHICAL, AND OPTICAL INSTRUMENTS
   Including clocks, chronometers, &c.

Class 15—MANUFACTURE OF METALS AND INSTRUMENTS THEREFOR
   Including furnaces, implements for casting, nail and screw machines, hardware, safes, cutlery, &c.

Class 16—NAVIGATION AND MARITIME IMPLEMENTS
   Comprising all vessels for conveyance on water, their construction, rigging, and propulsion; implements for fishing; diving-dresses, life-preservers, &c.

Class 17—STEAM AND GAS ENGINES
   Including boilers and furnaces therefor, and parts thereof

Class 18—STONE AND CLAY
   Including stone dressing, clay moulding and burning, mortar machines, &c.

Class 19—SURGICAL INSTRUMENTS
   Including trusses, dental instruments, bathing apparatus, &c.

Class 20—WEARING APPAREL
   Including instruments for manufacturing articles for the toilet, &c.

Class 21—WOOD, MACHINES, AND TOOLS FOR MANUFACTURING
   Including sawing, planing, mortising, shingle, and stave, carpenters' and coopers' implements, buildings, roofs, &c.

Class 22—MISCELLANEOUS

sible. The examiners must, for one thing, make a very thorough search of what has gone before. Often patents are upset when the courts have evidence of prior use or publication that the examiner did not know about.

In an effort to keep the standards of issued patents high and invalidation unlikely, the Office has conducted a "quality audit" program since 1967. After the applications have been allowed by the examiners, but before they go to the printer, the audit section takes a statistical sample. Applications in the sample are checked for quality in three areas: (1) practice and procedure, (2) the field of search and classification, and (3) judgments relating to patentability under the law.

The Filing System

With more than 3.5 million patents and 7.5 million foreign patents in existence, examiners have to know exactly where to look for earlier inventions. This has led to a classification system with more than 300 main classes and about 64,000 subclasses. The totals change, as the reclassification of patents goes on all the time.

A glance at the U.S. Patent Office classification list of 1838 (Chart II) illustrates the simplicity of the problem in an earlier day. Many of the terms in the original twenty-two classes of 1838 sound quaint to modern ears. By way of contrast, the first twenty-two classes (in an alphabetical arrangement) of the mid-1969 patent classes are listed below:

Abrading
Acoustics
Adhesive Bonding and Miscellaneous Chemical Manufacture
Advancing Material of Indeterminate Length
Aeronautics
Agitating
Ammunition and Explosive-Charge Making
Ammunition and Explosive Devices

Amplifiers
Amusement and Exercising Devices
Amusement Devices, Games
Amusement Devices, Toys
Animal Husbandry
Apparel
Apparel Apparatus
Article Dispensing
Artificial Body Members
Automatic Temperature and Humidity Regulation
Baggage
Baths, Closets, Sinks, and Spittoons
Batteries
Beds

In the elaborate modern system, the principal criterion that determines in which of the classes a patent is placed is the "fundamental, direct, or necessary utility" of the claimed invention. Within a selected class, subclass hierarchy determines the choice of subclass for placement. Subject matter that is disclosed but not made part of the patent claims is included, and cross-references are provided.

The loose-leaf *Manual of Classification* lists all the classes and subclasses, and gives other information. Except for Class 130 (Threshing), all class and subclass titles listed in the manual are defined. The definitions, along with supplementary search notes, are contained in fourteen loose-leaf volumes.

MECHANIZATION

In theory, the Patent Office should be able to put to its own use the vast computer technology in its files, so that an examiner could press a few buttons and have immediately spread before him a summary of all prior patents and publications bearing on an application. At least, he should be able to print out the patent numbers and the dates and sources of pertinent technical papers.

For fifteen years the subject of mechanized searching has been considered not only in the Patent Office but in the scientific and industrial communities. In 1954 an advisory committee headed by Dr. Vannevar Bush recommended to the Secretary of Commerce that machine-searching of compositions of matter (chemicals) be put on an operational basis, that a research and development unit be established in the Patent Office, and that the National Bureau of Standards and the Patent Office undertake a joint program to develop the necessary machines and techniques. Since then, the research and development unit has been set up, and joint programs have been carried out by the two agencies, including one called Project Haystaq.

Although probably nobody concerned (including members of congressional committees) is completely satisfied, some progress has been made, and the Patent Office has begun to use the computer in several ways. Potentially the most important use is for finding prior patents and pertinent publications. Employees in the Research and Development Division began searching various chemical subclasses by computer in 1969 at the request of examiners, and a good many groups in electronics were ready for the same procedure. But the volume was still small, perhaps no more than 1 or 2 per cent of the total number of searches.

An important start has also been made in the computer printing of patents and in compilation of a "data base" that may someday serve for mechanized searching. In a small way, photocomposition with magnetic tape storage and computer processing began in 1963 when the Patent Office published a pamphlet listing patent attorneys and agents. Six years later the List of Patentees index in the weekly *Official Gazette* was being set in a similar way. As will be explained in Chapter XI, the first printing of patents by the process was done in August, 1970, and the magnetic tape on which the applications had been recorded was transferred to storage in the new data base.

For the last twenty years, punched cards and sorting machines have been used in searching. Decks of punched cards covering such fields as steroids (the wonder drugs) and organo-metallic compounds are sold to industry for the use of company patent lawyers. In a related searching system, the "peek-a-boo" system, common characteristics of many patents can be detected by holding the cards up to the light. When the coded holes in the cards coincide, so do the characteristics. Cousins of the peek-a-boo are the microfilm cards known as CLIPS (Coincident Light Information Photographic Sheets). These have been used experimentally for checking many cards at once.

Sets of cards for some classes and subclasses have been prepared by the Patent Office for searching American patents only, and other sets covering foreign as well as domestic inventions have been made up in cooperation with ICIREPAT (International Cooperation in Information Retrieval Among Examining Patent Offices), an international committee whose members exchange data on patents in given fields. By 1969, the U.S. Patent Office was using an international file on lasers and masers, and another on analog-digital converters.

The data on many punched cards and peek-a-boo cards were also available in 1969 on the Patent Office computer. With the acquisition of additional equipment permitting time-sharing, which means that examiners can get answers at any hour without waiting, the computer will probably be given preference. Nearly all the 3.5 million patents have been recorded on microfilm so that, when the original supply of printed copies of any patent is exhausted, additional copies can be printed on photographic paper without resorting to the printing press.

Limited use has been made of "aperture cards," in lieu of paper copies of patents, for searching purposes. Each aperture card contains a 2-inch piece of 35-mm film, which can hold up to eight pages. The drawings and printed descriptions of the average patent will fit in a single card and can be examined in a desk viewer. About 10 per cent require two cards per patent, but very few need more. At this writing, it is expected that in time aperture cards will be in general use by the examiners and by lawyers, professional searchers, and inventors in the Public Search Room.

THE INVENTOR'S ROLE

The man or woman whose job, in whole or in part, is inventing for a corporation has few worries with regard to patenting. The company patent lawyer does the legal work, and the treasurer pays the fees. For his reward, the corporate inventor looks to promotion and any special compensation his employer grants. On the other hand, the independent inventor must hire an attorney, pay the attorney and the Patent Office, wait for his patent, and try to get income from it. It is true that some independents get their own patents without attorneys, but the Patent Office advises that inventors have professional help, because the procedures are complex. A practitioner may be found by consulting the *Directory of Registered Patent Attorneys and Agents,* published by the Patent Office and available from the Government Printing Office. A patent agent is not an attorney at law, but he is qualified to practice before the agency. The list is arranged by state and city.

For the independent, there are several necessary steps that precede the patent application. First, the inventor must decide whether his idea is practical, and worth the time and expense. Then he must keep complete records, preferably including a description and drawings and the date of conception, signed by two witnesses capable of understanding the invention.

A new Patent Office service for inventors, initiated in 1969 and already proving its popularity, is called the disclosure document program. A disclosure document, properly made out and mailed to the Office with a $10 fee, may be used as evidence of the date an invention was conceived. In the past, some inventors have tried to protect their conception priorities by mailing themselves registered letters and leaving them sealed, but this procedure was inadequate. The disclosure paper is kept on file for two years and then destroyed unless it is referred to in the inventor's patent application. The Patent Office emphasizes, however, that the document itself is not a patent application and that the date of its receipt does not become the date of a subsequent application.

A third preapplication step is the search, which may be performed by the inventor at the Patent Office Search Center but is usually done by a professional engaged by his attorney. The search may disclose a prior patent or technical publication proving the invention is not new and cannot be patented. If a study of related patents and publications obtained in the search indicates that a patent probably will be granted, the application may be filed.

An application for a patent includes a petition, a specification (description and claims), and an oath or declaration. If a patent is granted, the description and claims wind up as part of the text, although the claims may be greatly amended by exchanges between the examiner and the inventor or his attorney. The prescribed order for the specification is:

Title of the invention;
Abstract (a brief summary);
Cross references to related applications of the inventor or his associates;
Background of the invention, including its field and what has already been done in the field;
Summary of the invention;
Brief description of the drawings, with references to the figures by number;
Description of the preferred embodiment of the invention;
Claims (definitions of the invention and scope of protection).

After filing, there ensues what is called prosecution, involving exchanges of letters and telephone calls between the examiner and the attorney, and occasionally a personal interview, at which the inventor may be present. The examiner, who makes his own search, may find additional "prior art" that interferes with granting the application. The attorney tries to meet these objections by amending the claims, which may have been too broad, and, if he is successful, receives a notice of allowance. Upon payment of the final fee, the attorney gets a receipt giving the patent number and issue date assigned and can advise the inventor some weeks ahead of time when to expect the patent.

The Patent Office observes strict secrecy on pending applications. Owners, however, sometimes make inventions public prior to patent issuance if they feel confident that protection is not endangered. The manufacturer or seller of an article may also use the words "patent pending" or "patent applied for" if an application is on file. With these exceptions, it may be said that nothing is more secret than a pending patent and nothing is more public than an issued patent.

An inventor may become involved in an eventually costly dispute before or after the patent is issued, and the case may be carried all the way to the Supreme Court. Interferences go first to the Board of Patent Interferences in the Patent Office, and the Board's decisions may be appealed to the U.S. Court of Customs and Patent Appeals, or the loser may start a civil action against the winner in a U.S. District Court. An applicant whose patent claims are twice rejected has recourse to the Patent Office Board of Appeals. Its decision may be appealed to the U.S. Court of Customs and Patent Appeals, or the aggrieved person may start a civil action in the U.S. District Court for the District of Columbia against the Commissioner of Patents.

Once a patent is issued, someone may infringe it by using the invention without the owner's consent. The U.S. District

Courts have primary jurisdiction in infringement actions, whose costs often prove burdensome to independent inventors and small businessmen. Decisions that reach the Circuit Courts of Appeals from the District Courts, as well as those of the U.S. Court of Customs and Patent Appeals, are subject to review by the Supreme Court. The Patent Office does not serve as the inventor's lawyer, nor as his salesman. The agency does not recommend patent brokers or promoters. Field offices of the Department of Commerce and the Small Business Administration may be able to give advice locally on marketing inventions, and the Business and Defense Services Administration of the Department of Commerce in Washington may provide information and counsel as to development prospects in various industries.

THE PATENT DOCUMENT ITSELF

What does a patent look like? The term is usually applied to the printed document as distributed for 50 cents by the Patent Office. But the inventor or his assignee receives also, attached to his copy, an impressive sheet bearing the Commissioner's facsimile signature and reading as follows:

Whereas, there has been presented to the Commissioner of Patents a petition praying for the grant of Letters Patent for an alleged new and useful invention the title and description of which are contained in the specification of which a copy is hereunto annexed and made a part hereof, and the various requirements of Law in such cases made and provided have been complied with, and the title thereto is, from the records of the Patent Office in the Claimant(s) indicated in the said copy, and Whereas, upon due examination made, the said Claimant(s) is (are) adjudged to be entitled to a patent under the Law,

Now, therefore, these Letters Patent are to grant unto the said Claimant(s) and the successors, heirs or assigns of the said Claimant(s) for the term of Seventeen years from the date of this grant, subject to the payment of issue fees as provided by Law, the right to exclude others from making, using or selling the said Invention throughout the United States.

A patent picked at random, No. 3,430,482, granted in 1969 for an automatic bomb detector for airplanes, includes two sheets of drawings and three printed pages of description and claims. After the title (Automatic Bomb Detector) and the names of the two inventors (Andrew Dravnieks and Martin J. Salkowski) and the two assignees (the Secretary of the Army and the Administrator of the Federal Aviation Administration) are listed the filing date and the serial number assigned to the application. Then come the U.S. classification number and the international classification symbols. The U.S. number indicates where the patent and others like it are classified and filed under the Patent Office system. The international symbols (letters and figures) were added for the first time in January, 1969, and are intended to facilitate placing the patents in search files abroad.

The international classification had its genesis in a Working Party of Experts on Classification organized in 1952, under the Council of Europe. The experts included representatives from France, Holland, West Germany, and the United Kingdom. They adopted the basic scheme of the German patent classification system, in which the major subdivisions follow the branches of trade and industry. A modified version was adopted by the Council of Europe in 1954, revised in 1962, and updated in 1967.

The original sections, subsections, classes, and subclasses of the international system have been elaborated by dividing the subclasses into groups and subgroups. The system is not as refined as the American, but the symbols should be of value to Americans by giving them clues to where patents may be filed abroad in the future.

Another recent innovation in American patents is the abstract, which is intended to be a simple summary, about one hundred words long, to save time for researchers, including engineers and businessmen interested in the technology involved. In practice the abstract is not always clearly written, but when properly prepared it should tell the reader whether he needs to study the detailed disclosure and the claims at the end. The abstract in the automatic bomb detector patent cited above reads as follows:

> This invention relates to a bomb detector for identifying the presence of dynamite, for example, in an airplane. The basic method detects the presence of ethylene glycol dinitrate vapor in air. The essential steps are selective adsorption of the vapor on a surface, desorption of the vapor and a timed passage through a short, chromatographic partition column, followed by a passage through a vapor detector which emits an identifying signal.

Lay readers of patents usually find helpful the recital of the inventor's objects and the customary explanation of operation or of how the machine or process works. For the patent lawyer or the inventor who wonders whether an exact idea has been anticipated, a careful examination of the claims is a requisite. At the end of the patent are citations of U.S. and foreign patents that were studied by the examiners when they passed on the application, as well as cross-references to the U.S. classification. The names of the primary and assistant examiner who worked on the case also appear.

The patent cited above is in the general form that has become familiar in recent years. As will be mentioned in Chapter XI, however, when computerized printing of patents began on a limited scale in August, 1970, the Patent Office introduced a new format with a front page on which the abstract, one drawing, and certain reference data were collected as a convenient summary. It is expected that the front page will be adopted for all patents when computer printing becomes general.

OTHER KINDS OF PATENTS

The foregoing discussion refers primarily to invention (or utility) patents, which constitute the great bulk of those issued. But the Patent Office grants two other kinds: design patents and plant patents.

Design patents, of which nearly 225,000 have been issued since the class was authorized in 1842, protect appearance, not structure or operation. The law provides that whoever invents any new, original, and ornamental design for an article of manufacture may obtain a patent therefor. The term may be 3.5, 7, or 14 years (instead of the 17 years for invention patents). The filing fee for each is $20, and the issue fee is $10, $20, or $30, depending on the term.

A plant patent has a 17-year term and is granted to anyone who "invents or discovers and asexually reproduces any distinct and new variety of plant, including cultivated sports, mutants, hybrids, and newly found seedlings, other than a tuber-propagated plant or a plant found in an uncultivated state." (Asexually means not by seed, and the exclusion of tuber-propagated plants rules out the Irish potato and the Jerusalem artichoke.) The fees are the same as for invention patents. Only about 3,000 plant patents have been granted since they were authorized in 1930.

850,000 TRADEMARKS

Although patents are the agency's chief responsibility and its general center of interest, it administers another form of intellectual property—trademarks—which are of great importance to business. At one time it also registered a third form—copyrights—but for many years these have been handled by the Library of Congress.

The year 1970 marks the centennial of the U.S. trademark system, but it should be explained that the first statute, passed in 1870, was declared unconstitutional nine years later because it was based on the patent-copyright clause of the Constitution. In 1881 a successor law was adopted, which required use of the mark cither in commerce with foreign nations or with the Indian tribes. It was superseded in 1905 by a more comprehensive law that set up criteria for registrability and for the first time mentioned interstate commerce. The present trademark statute was passed in 1946.

Right to a trademark is established by its use in trade, and its owner may rely on state or common law, without federal registration. Such registration, however, is highly desirable as recognizing exclusive rights in interstate commerce.

Most applicants want to get their marks on the principal register, which is primarily for arbitrary, coined, fanciful, suggestive, or "invented" marks. "Kodak" is an example of such a mark. A supplemental register, which gives less legal protection, is provided for descriptive words, geographical names and surnames, slogans, labels, packages, and configurations of goods. There are also service marks, distinguishing services rather than goods; certification marks, intended to give assurance of quality or origin, and collective marks, indicating membership in a union or fraternity.

In all, the Patent Office has registered more than 850,000 marks, including names seen on every pantry shelf, as well as cattle brands and the sound of NBC's three-note chime. In recent years, the annual total of registrations has been more than 20,000, and renewals have been about 4,000. Trademarks remain in force for twenty years and can be renewed indefinitely if they are still in use and the fees are paid. A number have been in use for more than seventy-five years.

Examiners make a thorough search to see whether a mark for which application has been filed conflicts with prior registered marks or applications. Notice of an application for the principal register, if approved, is published in the *Official Gazette* for opposition, and objections to its registration may be filed within thirty days. In such notices, both the U.S. class in which it falls and the international classification, recognized by about seventy countries, are indicated. Registration on the supplemental register does not require notice for opposition. A handy introduction to the subject is the Patent Office publication *General Information Concerning Trademarks.*

THE BOOKKEEPING

One complaint of independent inventors is that the cost of obtaining a patent is too high. The principal expense lies in attorneys' charges, which are not regulated by the government and which, if there are interferences or litigation, may run high. At the present scale for Patent Office fees, the inventor or his employer pays a filing fee (except on designs) of $65, plus additional charges according to the number of claims and the manner of their presentation, and an issue fee of $100, plus $10 for each printed page and $2 for each sheet of drawings. The Patent Office has calculated its fees for a patent of average length and complexity at $229.

No tabulations of the total cost of getting a patent are available, but an informed guess is that, if there are no complications, the attorney may charge from $600 to $800, including the expense of preparing the drawings. For an average patent not involved in a dispute, therefore, the over-all outlay may be from $800 to $1,000.

As of June 30, 1931, it was calculated that the Patent Office since 1836 had made a profit of $5,616,827.78 on its activities. In most years between 1900 and 1934 the agency showed a profit, but 1934 proved to be its last year in the black. For thirty-five years thereafter the Patent Office has been in the red, spending more money than it takes in in fees. Its cash income is turned over to the Treasury, and the agency lives on appropriations. Recently the fees have offset nearly two-thirds of the operating cost, but in fiscal 1970, partly because of salary increases, the income amounted to only slightly over half of the expenses. For fiscal years 1965–69 the totals were:

Fiscal Year	Fees	Operating Cost
1965	$ 9,204,000	$31,258,000
1966	18,146,000	33,507,000
1967	23,666,000	35,534,000
1968	24,526,000	38,571,000
1969	25,456,000	42,576,000

Patent Office fees are fixed by Congress. Filing and issue fees, which now constitute more than half of the total receipts, were increased by law, effective October 25, 1965. The President's Commission on the Patent System, in its report filed in 1966 (see Appendix C), recommended that the Commissioner of Patents be authorized to set the fees "within broad guidelines established by Congress" and that they be apportioned in accordance with the cost of providing the services. A "patent reform" bill introduced to carry out the Commission's recommendations contained such a provision, but opposition developed in congressional committees, and it was dropped. In 1969, however, the Senate Judiciary Subcommittee on Patents, Trademarks, and Copyrights indicated that, inasmuch as it was contemplated when the fees were last adjusted in 1965 that the Patent Office should recover from two-thirds to three-fourths of its operating budget, the schedule should be given further consideration soon.

The Patent Office budget presented to Congress for fiscal 1970 was $46,110,000, including $1 million for additional printing and $890,000 for salaries of examiners to be added to the staff. The actual appropriation was $44,500,000, and the request for forty-two additional examiners to keep abreast of the patent intake was turned down. Supplemental funds asked and granted for two pay raises effective in fiscal 1970 brought the total to $48,684,000. The appropriation for 1971 was $52.2 million, subject to supplemental requests.

In 1968 the Patent Office announced a new "defensive publication" program for applicants who merely want to assure themselves the right to use an invention without carrying their cases through to issuance of a patent. An abstract of the pending application is printed without charge in the *Official Gazette* and the application itself is opened to the public. The applicant formally abandons his application, and it is not examined. Such disclosure is calculated to prevent anyone else from patenting the invention. The program enables the applicant to avoid paying an issue fee. It also relieves the Patent Office of work.

The principal duties of the Patent Office, then, include examining applications, issuing patents, maintaining a Patent Search Center for public use at its headquarters, and supplying a great deal of information on paper and microfilm to lawyers, inventors, businessmen, and the curious. Similiar services are performed with respect to trademarks.

Boards pass on patent interferences (disputes as to which inventor was first) and on appeals from the examiners' decisions. Miscellaneous Patent Office tasks are examining persons who want to practice before it as attorneys or agents (qualified nonlawyers), recording the assignments of patents and trademark rights, and exchanging ideas and data with patent officials around the world.

The staff is successful in keeping patent applications secret. And the inventor can get his full rights under the law without a letter from his congressman.

The Patent Office is the chief instrument that Dwight D. Eisenhower had in mind when he said, "Soundly based on the principle of protecting and rewarding inventors, this system has for years encouraged the imaginative to dream and to experiment—in garages and sheds, in great universities and corporate laboratories."

IV

Patents—Famous and Foolish

The millions of issued patents reflect inventors' motives and many of their human qualities. The principal motive is, of course, to make money, but there are others: to gain fame, to display ingenuity, to make a contribution to society—or just to beat the competition to it. Roughly half of all patented inventions are used at one time or another before the patents expire. A tiny trace of humor, sometimes conscious but usually unconscious, is enough to give the list a sparkle.

Often an invention shows an extreme concern for the comfort of man or beast. In recent years Americans have patented a burp seat for babies, a spanking paddle that breaks if daddy strikes too hard, and special toilet seats for dogs, cats, and even rabbits. Once discrimination raised its ugly head, when James Puckle of London obtained a royal patent in 1718 for a machine gun equipped with round bullets for Christians and square bullets for Turks. On the whole, however, patents are $99\frac{44}{100}$ per cent prosaic—and some are of immense importance.

Robert C. Watson, President Eisenhower's dignified Commissioner of Patents, used to ask a newspaper reporter from time to time, "Do we still issue funny patents?" There was something plaintive in the question. As a serious administrator and believer in the patent system, he hoped there weren't any funny ones in the thousand or so his office granted every week. He was doing his best to discourage the trivial and the frivolous. But the answer to his question was always Yes.

No matter how serious their intent, some patents can't help amusing some people. In 1959, for example, a chemist for the Wm. Wrigley Jr. Company, chewing gum manufacturer, was granted two patents for making false teeth to which chewing gum would not stick. The company had a perfectly real sales problem with people who would like to buy its product but were afraid to endanger their dentures. Yet for everybody under the age of forty the invention conjured up a comic picture.

Trade procedures, although governed by solid considerations, are often amusing—if it's somebody else's trade. A machine that squirts jelly into jelly doughnuts performs a legitimate industrial function. To an outsider, even though he loves jelly doughnuts, the operation nevertheless seems a little absurd. Some patents become quaint with the passage of time. The special "drink collector" for Prohibition agents of the 1920's seems dated nowadays. The ear trumpet that could be stowed away in a tall hat now seems old-fashioned. So do the mustache guards devised to facilitate the neat ingestion of soup—until we realize that the new generation may need them too. In some cases we smile because we think we know the things wouldn't work. An example is a patented nineteenth-century cannon that was designed to produce rain and to prevent hailstorms, tornadoes, droughts, frosts, and forest and prairie fires.

The Patent Office does not consciously grant patents for perpetual motion, but the long list contains a number not so represented—that is, for machines with no outside source of power but for which perpetual motion was not claimed. One was Patent 257,103, issued in 1882 to J. Sutliff, Sr., for an arrangement of wheels connected to a lever and ball in a tank of water.

Famous names appear among the patentees. In 1849 Abraham Lincoln, then in Congress, got Patent 6,469 for A Device for Buoying Vessels over Shoals. Mark Twain (Samuel L. Clemens) patented in 1871 An Improvement in Adjustable and Detachable Straps for Garments. Later he received patents for a self-pasting scrapbook and for a game to help players remember important historical dates. In recent years the inventors' lists have included some inventors in public life, such as Harold E. Stassen, often a candidate for office, and Representative Joseph Y. Resnick of New York state. In 1970 several names of noninventors appeared incidentally on the lists, as when a Washington sculptress and her son got design patents for statuettes of George C. Wallace, Richard M. Nixon, and Edward M. Kennedy.

The entertainment profession is represented by, among others, Zeppo Marx, inventor of a wrist alarm for persons subject to heart attacks. John Gary holds several patents for swimmers' equipment. Design patents have been granted to Lawrence Welk (lunch boxes), Danny Kaye (a blow-out toy), and Edie Adams (ring-shaped cigarette and cigar holders). Paul Winchell, the ventriloquist, has both invention and design patents. In 1942 Hedy Lamarr, the movie actress, and George Antheil, the composer, patented a "secret communication system." In earlier years Natacha Rambova, Rudolph Valentino's onetime leading lady, patented a doll that also served as a wrap or carriage robe. Lillian Russell patented a lighted dresser trunk, and Harry Houdini a diver's suit.

Besides the inventions that necessity was not the mother of, many patented products and processes have greatly benefited American technology and the American standard of living.

FAMOUS PATENTS

Lists of "great" patented inventions change with the years. The transistor and laser are recent additions. In 1940 a committee celebrating the U.S. patent law sesquicentennial selected nineteen outstanding great inventions and forty inventions of outstanding merit. In 1961, when the modern patent system had just turned 125, an unofficial list of "Ten Patents That Shaped the World" was published in the *New York Times Magazine*. The inventors, the inventions, and the patent years were:

Alexander Graham Bell: *Telephone,* No. 174,465, 1876
Thomas Alva Edison: *Incandescent Electric Lamp,* No. 223,898, 1880
Orville and Wilbur Wright: *Flying Machine,* No. 821,393, 1906
Lee De Forest: *First Three-Electrode Vacuum Tube,* No. 841,387, 1907
Leo H. Baekeland: *Moldable Plastics* (Bakelite), No. 942,809, 1909
William M. Burton: *Oil Cracking,* No. 1,049,667, 1913
Robert H. Goddard: *Rocket,* No. 1,102,653, 1914
Wallace H. Carothers: *Nylon,* No. 2,071,250, 1937
Selman A. Waksman and Albert Schatz: *Streptomycin,* No. 2,449,866, 1948
Enrico Fermi and Leo Szilard: *Atomic Reactor* (invented 1942), No. 2,708,656, 1955

The Department of Commerce has issued a list of twenty-two famous single inventors and the inventions most often associated with their names. This list is reproduced as Table II. Among the many other notable patents issued to single inventors or inventor teams not mentioned so far, the following should not be overlooked:

Whitcomb L. Judson: *Clasp Locker or Unlocker for Shoes* (the first zipper), No. 504,038, 1893
King C. Gillette: *Razor* (safety), No. 775,134, 1904
John Bardeen and Walter H. Brattain: *Three-Electrode Circuit Element Utilizing Semiconductive Materials* (point contact transistor), No. 2,524,035, 1950

William Shockley: *Circuit Element Utilizing Semiconductor Material* (junction transistor), No. 2,569,347, 1951

Robert C. Baumann: *Satellite Structure* (the Navy's pioneer Vanguard satellite), No. 2,835,548, 1958

Charles H. Townes: *Production of Electromagnetic Energy* (maser), No. 2,879,439, 1959

Arthur L. Schawlow and Charles H. Townes: *Masers and Maser Communications System* (laser), No. 2,929,922, 1960

HUMOR IN THE FILES

A favorite with those who collect amusing patents is No. 556,248, granted in 1896 to James C. Boyle of Spokane for a self-tipping hat. His purpose was laudable: to enable a man with his arms full of packages to salute a lady by merely nodding. The owner was to wind the mechanism and settle the derby firmly on his head. Then, when he bowed, the hat tipped forward, swung in a complete circle and settled back in place, to the amazement and admiration of onlookers.

Other patents draw a smile because the passage of time and the progress of science have made them seem naïve—we think we know better today. Alpheus Myers, M.D., who practiced in Logansport, Cass County, Indiana, probably caused a flutter among his fellow practitioners with a patent (No. 11,942) that he got in 1854. He announced it as a new and useful Trap for Removing Tapeworms from the Stomach and Intestines.

My invention [he wrote] consists in a trap which is baited, attached to a string, and swallowed by the patient after a fast of suitable duration to make the worm hungry. The worm seizes the bait, and its head is caught in the trap, which is then withdrawn from the patient's stomach by the string which has been left hanging from the mouth, dragging after it the whole length of the worm.

Dr. Myers explained that the trap consisted of a cylindrical box, to be made of gold, platinum, or other metal not easily

TABLE II

FAMOUS SINGLE INVENTORS AND THE INVENTIONS
MOST OFTEN ASSOCIATED WITH THEIR NAMES

Inventor	Invention and Patent Number	Date
Eli Whitney	Cotton Gin (unnumbered)	March 14, 1794
Cyrus Hall McCormick	Reaper (unnumbered)	June 21, 1834
Samuel F. B. Morse	Telegraph (No. 1,647)	June 20, 1840
Charles Goodyear	Preparing Fabrics of . . . India Rubber (vulcanized rubber) (No. 3,633)	June 15, 1844
Elias Howe, Jr.	Sewing Machines (No. 4,750)	September 10, 1846
Abraham Lincoln (whose patent was never put to use)	A Device [bellows] for Buoying Vessels over Shoals (No. 6,469)	May 22, 1849
Samuel Colt	Revolver (No. 20,144)	May 4, 1858
Richard J. Gatling	Revolving Battery Gun (No. 36,836)	November 4, 1862
George Westinghouse, Jr.	Steam-Power Brake Device (No. 88,929)	April 13, 1869
Joseph F. Glidden	Barbed Wire (No. 157,124)	November 24, 1874
Alexander Graham Bell	Telephone (No. 174,465)	March 7, 1876
Thomas Alva Edison (who was granted 1,093 patents)	Phonograph (No. 200,521) Incandescent Lamp (No. 223,898)	February 19, 1878 January 27, 1880
Elihu Thomson	Apparatus for Electrical Welding (No. 347,140)	August 10, 1886
Nikola Tesla	Electrical Transmission of Power (Electric Motor) (No. 382,280)	May 1, 1888
Charles M. Hall	Manufacture of Aluminum (No. 400,665)	April 2, 1889
Ottmar Mergenthaler	Linotype (No. 436,532)	September 16, 1890
Guglielmo Marconi (Italian citizen)	Wireless Telegraphy (No. 586,193)	July 13, 1897
Rudolph Diesel (of Berlin, Germany)	Internal-Combustion Engine (No. 608,845)	August 9, 1898
Henry Ford	Carburetor (No. 610,040) Motor Carriage (No. 686,046)	August 30, 1898 November 5, 1901
Ferdinand Zeppelin (of Stuttgart, Germany)	Navigable Balloons (No. 621,195)	March 14, 1899
Michael J. Owens	Glass Shaping Machine for Bottles, Jars, etc. (No. 766,768)	August 2, 1904
Leo H. Baekeland	Condensation Products and Method of Making Same (led to Bakelite and plastics) (No. 942, 809)	December 7, 1909

corroded, and with a rounded cap to which the cord was attached. In one side was an opening of sufficient size for the worm's head to be introduced. The trap was to be baited with "any nutritious substance." A metal jaw with teeth was to catch the worm when it touched the bait. Dr. Myers cautioned that, in constructing the trap, care should be taken that the spring be only strong enough to hold the worm and not strong enough to cut off its head.

Many an inventor has shown conscious humor. Take, for example, Thomas Windell of New Albany, Indiana, who in 1860 was granted No. 28,029 for a tombstone made of glass in which inscriptions might be pressed. The patent drawings display this epitaph:

> Here lies Windell
> An inventor by trade,
> This Monument you see
> Is an invention he made
>
> *   *   *
>
> A curious fact
> It has sometimes been said
> That he made it while living,
> But enjoys it while dead

For the dentist's office, William M. Butler of San Francisco patented in 1865 (No. 51,552) a spittoon that would catch gold fillings. When the patient whose teeth were being filled expectorated, Mr. Butler said, the particles of gold and silver would amalgamate with mercury at the mouth of the spittoon. The cuspidor was fitted with a universal joint for convenient manipulation, and Mr. Butler asserted that it would form a unique and neat appendage for any dentist's chair.

Two Newark inventors, Zadoc P. Dederick and Isaac Grass, were granted a patent in 1868 for their Steam-Carriage, which consisted of an engine shaped like a man, pulling a cart. The pseudo-human figure in the drawings of this patent (No. 75,874) is shown walking briskly, wearing a top hat and smoking a pipe. A boiler constitutes the torso, and the steam piston underneath is connected by a series of rods to the jointed legs. The patent explains, in part, that "the foot is turned down at the toe as one leg falls behind the other, and the knee bent, so that as the foot is thrown forward, it is raised by bending the knee, to step over any obstacle, the foot being turned downwards at the toe before being placed on the ground."

Twenty years later, in 1888, Jack William James of Cuba, Tennessee, was awarded Patent 386,403, on Apparatus for Preventing Collisions of Railway Trains. One feature was a dummy, seated on a flat car ahead of the engine, that rang a gong with each revolution of the wheels for the purpose of frightening cattle from the track and announcing the approach of a train. In front of the flat car was a pole, supported by wheels. When the pole struck a train coming from the opposite direction, or some object like a log, a man's body, or a cow, an electric connection would apply the airbrakes, reverse the engine, and pull in the flat car.

An Improvement in Fire-Escapes, patented (No. 221,855) in 1879 by Benjamin B. Oppenheimer of Trenton, Tennessee, consisted of a parachute and thickly padded shoes. The patent illustration shows a man of serious demeanor with his hands clasped in front of his chest and his coattails flying. The parachute is overhead, and the man's weight rests on a strap beneath his chin.

A device for inducing sleep, patented in 1885 by Fanny W. Paul of New York City, surely attracted the attention of the medical fraternity. It was a collar to be tightened around the neck in order to cut down the circulation of blood to the head —to a point somewhere short of strangulation. Patent 313,516 explained that the user was to hold it on for from ten to twenty minutes. By thus regulating the pressure on his jugular vein and arteries and reducing the activity of his brain, he would become more and more relaxed and finally lapse into refreshing slumber.

Aeronauts of the 1880's were shown by Charles Richard Edouard Wulff of Paris how to propel and guide balloons by harnessing birds. His patent (No. 363,037), granted in 1887, described the equipment. It consisted of corsets to hold eagles, vultures, or condors to a movable framework. By shifting the framework, an attendant could direct where the birds were to fly. When the balloon was to be stationary, a net would restrain the wings of the birds.

Beauty aids have long intrigued inventors. In Patent 560,351, Martin Goetze of Berlin, Germany, presented in 1896 a device for producing dimples. It resembled a brace and bit, with a massage knob made of ivory, marble, celluloid, or India rubber where the bit would be. The knob was to be placed on the spot at which a dimple was desired. When the brace was turned, the knob would depress the spot while a massage cylinder moved around it, making the skin malleable.

An alarm-bed patented (No. 643,789) by Ludwig Ederer of Omaha, Nebraska, in 1900 was designed to waken the night attendant at a hothouse or conservatory when the pressure in the steam pipes dropped too low. A pipe diaphragm released a catch on the bed so that the foot end fell to the floor, reminding the sleeper that it was time to replenish the fire.

For the sportsman, William P. Zeigler of Ambridge, Pennsylvania, patented in 1916 an artificial fish bait with a mirror. He explained in Patent 1,180,753 how it worked:

> A male fish seeing his image upon looking therein will appear to see another fish approach it from the opposite side with the intent to seize the bait, and this will not only arouse his warlike spirit, but also appeal to his greed, and he will seize the bait quickly in order to defeat the approaching rival. . . . In the case of a female fish the attractiveness of a mirror is too well known to need discussion. Thus the bait appeals to the ruling

passion of both sexes, and renders it very certain and efficient in operation.

Two relatively recent inventions evidence concern for pets: A diaper for parakeets, patented (No. 2,882,858) by Bertha A. Dlugi of Detroit in 1959, and a toothbrush for dogs, patented (No. 3,007,441) by Bird A. Eyer of Seattle in 1961. Notable among the bathroom innovations recorded in the Patent Office files is a vibrating toilet seat, conceived by Thomas J. Bayard, proprietor of a Chicago hair studio for men, and protected in 1966 by Patent 3,244,168. There are many other bathroom (and bedroom) patents that attorneys keep in their desks to amuse visiting clients. Among the milder items is an old-fashioned time signal for water closets that was intended by its inventor to prevent employees from malingering during work hours. With the coming of the motor age, another inventor designed a commode for automobiles.

The question may arise as to why some patents were granted for ideas that now seem comic. The answer is that the applications met, or seemed to the examiners to meet, the laws and regulations of the time. The Patent Office is not required to judge whether a patentee can make money from his concept; if it seems plausible, it often gets by, although it may never work. Two patents were issued early in 1970 for methods of producing power by atomic fusion (as distinct from fission), although the scientists who applied had not succeeded in generating any power.

No computer and no corporation as such can obtain a U.S. patent. Inventors are all people, and it is small wonder that their ideas mirror human aspirations and often provide good fun—most of it clean, some of it borderline.

PATENT SUITS AND DISPUTES

Lawsuits arising from disputes over patents have been capturing headlines in the United States for more than a century.

Three of the most famous of these are the series of suits and disputes over the materials and processes used in false teeth, the so-called Telephone Cases, and the suits arising over the Selden patent of 1895, which collected tribute from the young automotive industry until it was successfully challenged by a manufacturer of horseless carriages named Henry Ford.

Patents and False Teeth

Charles Goodyear received Patent No. 3,633 in 1844 for an Improvement in the Manner of Preparing Fabrics of Caoutchouc or India-Rubber. His process for the vulcanization of rubber proved a boon to dentists, who used vulcanite in making baseplates and paid royalties until the original Goodyear patents had expired. But what was known as "the Cummings patent," granted in 1864, covered the *process* of making rubber baseplates, and the Goodyear Dental Vulcanite Company compelled dentists to take out licenses and pay royalties under this patent. Millions of dollars were involved, and half the dental profession was reportedly bankrupted; other practitioners avoided payment by using celluloid.

About 1868, control of the patents fell into the hands of Josiah Bacon, treasurer of a Boston rubber company. He exacted annual fees for the use of vulcanite ranging from $25 to $100 a year, depending on the size of the practice, plus $1 per denture of five teeth or fewer, and $2 for six teeth or more. The terms were accepted by about 5,000 dentists. Intimidation, lawsuits, and fines were employed to enforce the tribute. In 1879 an irate dentist, Samuel P. Chalfont, killed Bacon in a San Francisco hotel. Although Dr. Chalfont was sentenced to ten years, his bullet put an end to the persecution of the profession, and the patents expired in 1881.

The relief did not last long. A new concern, the International Tooth Crown Company, was formed and bought between thirty-five and fifty patents on gold crowns, on the backing or soldering of facings, and on other dental devices and processes. By 1886 the company was issuing licenses, demanding payments, and suing practitioners. The fees for the right to practice crown and bridge work under the patents ranged from $100 to $500 a year. The Dental Protective Association, organized and financed through the efforts of Dr. J. N. Crouse of Chicago, a former president of the American Dental Association, contested the International Tooth Crown Company's patents in court, but it was not until 1900 that the last of the crown and bridge patents had been invalidated.

Later the Dental Protective Association and Dr. Crouse were to switch sides and attempt to enforce the claims of another inventor, himself a dentist. Dr. William Taggart of Chicago had demonstrated his gold-inlay process at a professional meeting in New York in 1907 and received a patent late that year for his Method for Making Molds for Dental Inlays and the Like. His casting process was hailed as freeing the dental profession from the hard work of gold-foil operations, but he was slow in getting his $110 casting machine on the market and was outdistanced by rival manufacturers.

Dr. Taggart then tried other ways to cash in on the process he had invented. He brought infringement suits against dentists in the District of Columbia and Chicago. Dr. Crouse's Dental Protective Association circularized all members of the profession, offering them for $25 both membership in the association and the right to use the process. In opposition, a Dentist Protective Alliance was formed on a national scale, and lawsuits followed. Finally, in 1911, a United States District Court was convinced that an Iowa dentist had produced metal inlays for his patients as early as 1896, and the Taggart patents were invalidated.

The work of the Dentist Protective Alliance was later turned over to the American Dental Association, which has continued its vigilance against process patents. The association's *Journal,* in the centennial historical issue, published in

June, 1959, concluded an account of the long litigation with these words:

> The general knowledge that organized dentistry is ready to defend itself against exploitation by means of process patents no doubt will continue to discourage effectively attempts at such exploitation. This is one of the many solid achievements that the organized dental profession in the United States can celebrate in its centennial year.

The Yellow Breeches Telephone

As every schoolboy knows, Alexander Graham Bell invented the telephone and transmitted a complete sentence over his instrument on March 10, 1876, three days after the granting of his basic patent. The sentence was, "Mr. Watson, come here, I want you!" Yet if one Supreme Court Justice had changed his mind in 1888, today's schoolchildren might be memorizing instead the rags-to-riches story of one Daniel Drawbaugh. A "cloud of witnesses" had testified in the lower court that Drawbaugh, a penniless mechanic, had talked over his homemade instruments in the 1860's and early 1870's. His first transmitter was a teacup, and his receiver a tin can.

Bell's company, the American Bell Telephone Company, was not without rivals for long. A group of promoters, described in the newspapers as Washington and Cincinnati capitalists, organized the People's Telephone Company under New York laws, with authorized capital of $5 million. They proposed to manufacture telephones under patents issued to Frank A. Klemm and Abner G. Tisdel—and under applications for patents filed by Drawbaugh in 1880. When the promoters of the new company had discovered Drawbaugh, he was gaining his living by doing odd jobs at Eberly's Mills, sometimes called Milltown, a cluster of houses in Cumberland

County near Harrisburg, Pennsylvania, on the bank of a stream named Yellow Breeches Creek.

In the same year that Drawbaugh's applications were filed, the American Bell Telephone company sued Drawbaugh's associates for infringement. By then 100,000 Bell telephones and many thousands of miles of line were paying royalties to the Bell company, and Bell's "speaking telephone" was already four years old, having been exhibited at the Philadelphia Centennial Exposition in 1876. Drawbaugh's teacup/tin solidus can device was said to be nine years its senior.

Daniel Drawbaugh had been born at Eberly's Mills July 14, 1827. As a boy, he helped his father in the family blacksmith shop. Until he grew tall enough to reach the bellows handle, father stood him on a box. His formal education was confined to five winters, or fewer, in a rural school. As a lad he made a number of inventions, including a machine for sawing wagon wheel rims.

In the winter of 1859–60 Professor Samuel B. Heiges delivered a series of lectures on physics at a school near Eberly's Mills. Drawbaugh, who attended the lectures, told Heiges he thought it would be possible to transmit speech over a telegraph wire. In 1867 Drawbaugh told James A. Smith, postmaster at New Cumberland, that he had talked to his daughter Emma when they were separated by a floor and two partitions. He gave Smith the impression that it was done by wire. Drawbaugh's first transmitter was a teacup with a membrane, powered by a battery. His first receiver was a tin can with bottom and top removed and also fitted with a membrane. In 1867, also, Samuel Snell heard "words . . . pretty distinctly" over a line from the shop to the grist mill on Yellow Breeches Creek. A glass tumbler had succeeded the porcelain teacup as the transmitter, according to testimony, and the tin receiver had been improved. In 1869 A. B. Shank heard and understood words spoken into the transmitter and recognized Drawbaugh's voice. Soon magnetic instruments succeeded the battery machine.

Drawbaugh's struggles against poverty were portrayed in the voluminous testimony for the District Court trial, most of which was taken by deposition in Harrisburg. He hadn't had the money for patents on his telephone. The Civil War bankrupted him, as he could not collect for the stave-making machinery he had sold in the South. From 1867 to 1870, his net income for himself and his family from odd jobs was about $22 per month, or 75 cents a day.

Between 300 and 400 witnesses were produced to establish Drawbaugh's priority. In their testimony, the date February 14, 1876, was highly important, because on that day Bell had filed application for his first telephone patent. In a brief for the appeal, attorneys for the People's Telephone Company said:

Upon reviewing the whole of the evidence, . . . it appears that 220 persons testify to knowledge of Mr. Drawbaugh's speaking telephone prior to February 14, 1876! Of these 141 actually saw the instruments, and the majority of them identify the particular machines which they saw; and about 70 heard talk through the machines or were present when others were successfully talking through them. The great majority of these witnesses testify to facts occurring prior to June 2, 1875, and therefore anticipating Bell's first alleged telephone experiments. . . .

It will be shown that, about [February 14, 1876] and from time to time thereafter, down to 1879, new telephones appeared in Mr. Drawbaugh's shop, of greatly improved form and construction, far in advance of all improvements made by other inventors.

Drawbaugh was his own worst witness. He had no records worth the name, "not further than that I used to make plans on drafting boards for working by." The case of *Bell* v. *People's* was decided in District Court at New York in 1884, and after a rehearing the decision was reaffirmed in 1885. The lower court found that Bell's patents were valid and had been infringed by People's Telephone Company and others. The consolidated cases reached the United States Supreme Court in 1887.

When the Supreme Court decision was rendered in 1888, a new member of the court, who had not heard the argument, took no part. Another disqualified himself for reasons of propriety. Chief Justice Morrison Remick Waite was ill, and asked Justice Samuel Blatchford to read the decision for him. After the hearing, Waite went home to bed. He died four days later. The decision was four to three in favor of the American Bell Telephone Company.

The majority opinion—in which Chief Justice Waite was joined by Justices Blatchford, Stanley Matthews, and Samuel Freeman Miller—recited the People's Telephone Company's contention that Drawbaugh had transmitted articulate vocal sounds and speech between distant points from 1870 through 1874. Between 300 and 400 witnesses had been produced to establish the priority of Drawbaugh's invention. His explanation of his failure to file for patents on his telephone was poverty. Yet, said the court, Drawbaugh had been much occupied early in 1876 with his electric clock and his measuring faucet for grocers to use in selling oil and molasses. The Chief Justice could not believe that Drawbaugh would not have filed patent applications for his telephone inventions, if they then existed, instead of for the clock and faucet. Two series of experiments with reproductions of old Drawbaugh instruments had been made in the lower court, but the Justice was not impressed with the record.

The court's opinion concluded: "Without pursuing the subject further we decide that the Drawbaugh defence has not been made out."

Justice Joseph F. Bradley, who was joined by Justices Stephen Johnson Field and John Marshall Harlan, vigorously disagreed. Justice Bradley wrote, in the minority opinion:

We think that Drawbaugh anticipated the invention of Mr. Bell, who, at most, is not claimed to have invented the speaking telephone prior to June 10, 1875. We think that the evidence on this point is so overwhelming, with regard both to the number and character of the witnesses, that it cannot be overcome. . . .

We are satisfied from a very great preponderance of evidence, that Drawbaugh produced, and exhibited in his shop, as early as 1869, an electrical instrument by which he transmitted speech, so as to be distinctly heard and understood, by means of a wire and the employment of variable resistance to the electrical current. . . .

We are also satisfied that as early as 1871 he reproduced articulate speech, at a distance, by means of a current of electricity, subjected by electrical induction to undulations corresponding to the vibrations of the voice in speaking,—a process substantially the same as that which is claimed in Mr. Bell's patent.

On the morning after the decision, the *New York Times* carried the headline

THE BELL MONOPOLY SAFE

A petition for rehearing was denied and what lawyers called for many years the Telephone Cases became history.

Drawbaugh missed national acclaim by one man's decision: If any of the four justices who sided with Bell had taken Drawbaugh's part, the Bell patents would have been invalidated. As Drawbaugh had delayed filing his application until more than the statutory two years after issuance of the Bell patents, he could not have obtained a valid patent in any event, and the telephone might have gone into the public domain. But besides the honor of being the first inventor,

Drawbaugh might have achieved prosperity through his association with the People's Telephone Company. The Bell Company (which is now the American Telephone and Telegraph Company) was not yet free of trouble. In all, it brought or fought 600 actions, including a Patent Office interference involving inventions by Elisha Gray and Thomas A. Edison. After the decision, Drawbaugh lost interest in inventing. He held a number of patents on telephone inventions dated later than Bell's and on other machines. His last years are reported to have been comfortable. He died November 3, 1911, at the age of 84.

Selden and the Horseless Carriage

A sensational case in the early 1900's involved George B. Selden's patent, which purported to cover the automobile. Most of the young motor car industry paid tribute; total royalties have been estimated at $5.8 million and Selden's share at more than $200,000. The one successful hold-out was Henry Ford, who in 1911 won on appeal an infringement action begun against him eight years before.

Selden was not an automotive engineer but a patent attorney who practiced in Rochester, New York. On May 8, 1879, he filed an application for an automotive patent, and by amending it from time to time kept it pending for sixteen years. The model that he supplied to the Patent Office was transferred many years later to the Smithsonian's National Museum.

Patent No. 549,160 was granted Selden on November 5, 1895. One of the witnesses who signed the patent drawings was George Eastman, inventor of the Kodak. The patent disclosed an automobile with a clutch, foot-brake, muffler, front-wheel drive, a power shaft arranged to run faster than the propelling wheel, and a "liquid hydrocarbon gas engine of the compression type." The type of engine proved important in the final court decision.

Four years after he received the patent, Selden sold control of it to the Columbia Motor Car Company, later known as the Electric Vehicle Company, which manufactured electric automobiles in Hartford, Connecticut. In 1900 the company entered suit for infringement against the Winton Motor Carriage Company. Three years later Winton capitulated and took a Selden license. In that same year the Association of Licensed Automobile Manufacturers was formed by ten companies paying royalties to Columbia. Others joined later.

The licensed companies agreed to pay a royalty of 1¼ per cent of the retail list price on all cars sold. The scale was later cut to 1 per cent and then to four-fifths of 1 per cent. At its height, the membership comprised 87 per cent of the American motor car industry and produced more than 90 per cent of the gasoline cars being built.

Before he incorporated the Ford Motor Company on June 16, 1903, Henry Ford considered taking a Selden license but was turned down, apparently as a poor risk. On July 23 of that year the first Ford Company car, a two-cylinder Model A, was sold. On October 22, Electric Vehicle and Selden filed an infringement suit against the Ford Company and others. Ford advertised that he would indemnify his customers against suits by the Selden interests and later posted the entire assets of his company (which were then far from substantial) as a bond.

As an exhibit, Selden had a car built embodying his patent, and Henry Ford had one built that incorporated an engine first patented in 1860 by a Frenchman, Jean Joseph Etienne Lenoir. According to Ford historians, the Selden car failed miserably and the Ford-Lenoir car performed beautifully for its time. Ford's purpose was to show that Selden had not patented a workable car and that, even if he had, it was not the first workable automobile patented. However, the United States District Court for the Southern District of New York ruled in favor of Selden, holding on September 15, 1909, that several of his claims had been infringed. Most of the Ford co-defendants joined the association, but Henry stood firm and appealed the decision.

On January 9, 1911, the Circuit Court of Appeals for the Second Circuit reversed the District Court, and Ford's long fight was won. The decision hinged on types of motors. Although the old Lenoir engine was literally out of the running (at the time of the litigation all automobiles were being propelled by Otto engines), Selden's patent was held to be valid for Brayton engines only. It had not been infringed because nobody by that time was using Brayton engines. Of Selden's approach to the patent, the court said:

> The Brayton engine was the leading engine of the time, and his attention was naturally drawn to its supposed advantages. He chose that type. In the light of events we can see that had he appreciated the superiority of the Otto engine and adapted that type for his combination his patent would cover the modern automobile. He did not do so.

The Selden interests did not try to carry the case to the Supreme Court, perhaps because the patent was to expire the following year, 1912. The Association of Licensed Automobile Manufacturers was dissolved. The cost to all hands of the eight-year patent lawsuit has been put at more than a million dollars—a far from insignificant figure for those days.

V

The International Picture

Spokesmen for both government and industry have chosen as the ultimate goal in the protection of inventions a universal patent, effective throughout the world. The President's Commission on the Patent System, appointed by Lyndon B. Johnson in 1965, issued a report the following year (see Appendix C), in which it expressed its belief in such a goal. The universal patent, it said, should be "issued in the light of, and inventive over, all of the prior art of the world, and obtained quickly and inexpensively on a single application, but only in return for a genuine contribution to the progress of the useful arts."

To this end the commission specifically recommended the pursuit of (1) international harmonization of patent practice, (2) the formation of regional patent system groups, and (3) a universal network of mechanized information storage and retrieval systems.

Before the commission's report was issued, David Sarnoff, chairman of RCA Corporation, in a 1966 address at George Washington University, cited the advances in communications as making an international patent framework possible. "It is now technically feasible," he said, "to establish a universal patent system, utilizing the latest communications devices and concepts, to bring swiftness, order, and reasonable uniformity to the entire patent structure." General Sarnoff asked:

When we can transmit an [inventive] idea around the world in less than one-seventh of a second, why must years elapse before that idea can be validated within or outside the country of origin? Why must an inventor still make separate application in every country where he wishes to protect his idea? Why should some countries make no provision at all for patent filings, or impose severely restrictive conditions upon the inventor?

The answers to these questions, as General Sarnoff saw them, lay in the fragmented array of national patent systems. He regarded as practical a world patent center that could receive and process applications from inventors everywhere. A few major patent countries could begin the operation shortly, and later other nations could join.

The burden of filing applications for patents on a single invention in many countries with as many different codes rests most heavily on companies doing an international business. The biggest corporations resent the paper work and expense but are able to afford them. The head of a relatively small American engineering firm complained in 1968 of losing out to a larger foreign competitor that was able to invest $1 million to protect a single invention in the fifty countries where a market appeared promising.

Americans filed 67,000 patent applications in the U.S. Patent Office in 1968; another 26,000 applications originated abroad. Of the 67,000 applications made in the U.S., nearly 25,000 were the basis of some 127,000 foreign filings. A projection indicated that in 1970 American inventions would result in 150,000 filings abroad, often in as many as fifteen or twenty countries.

THE PARIS CONVENTION

A universal patent is admittedly years away, but progress has been made toward two minor and nearer goals: (1) a unified procedure for obtaining patents in many countries on the same invention and (2) a single patent good in half a dozen countries.

International cooperation in the protection of inventions and trademarks began with the 1883 Paris Convention for the Protection of Industrial Property, to which the United States adhered in 1887. "Industrial property" in this sense includes patents, trademarks, industrial designs, utility models ("petty patents" issued in a few countries), trade names (designations under which business is carried on), and indications of source or origin.

Under the Paris Convention, each member country guarantees to the nationals of each other member the same treatment it gives its own citizens with regard to industrial property. Priority of filing is also recognized in other member states if applications are filed within a year (six months for designs and trademarks). Thus an inventor who files a patent application first in his own country can apply within a year in another member country and have his original date of filing recognized there. A filing date is more important in many other countries than it is in the United States, which recognizes the inventor who was first to invent, rather than the first to file.

The member countries also undertake to provide protection against unfair competition, including false allegations that may discredit the establishment, the goods, or the industrial or commercial activities of a competitor.

By the end of 1968, seventy-eight countries, including the Soviet Union, had joined the international union (the Paris Union) established by the 1883 convention. (The number was seventy-nine where East Germany was recognized as a state. The United States and numerous other members of the Paris Convention reject the contention that the East German regime is a member.)

THE PATENT COOPERATION TREATY

Delegations from fifty-four member countries of the Paris Union negotiated a Patent Cooperation Treaty at a diplomatic conference held in Washington from May 25 to June 19, 1970. It was the first international diplomatic conference on the subject of patents to be held in Washington since 1911, when the convention establishing the Paris Union was amended. Since the United States was host, an appropriation of $150,000 was made to the State Department for the purpose, in accordance with a joint congressional resolution adopted in 1969. The co-chairmen of the U.S. delegation were Deputy Assistant Secretary of State Eugene M. Braderman and Commissioner of Patents William E. Schuyler, Jr.

The treaty had been in preparation for four years. At the suggestion of the United States, the secretariat in Geneva that administers the Paris and other conventions had prepared a first draft, published in 1967. A revised version of this draft was considered the next year by a committee of experts, headed by Mr. Braderman, and the final negotiating draft was published in July, 1969. The final Patent Cooperation Treaty, the text of which was unanimously approved early in the conference, was adopted subject to ratification by the governments concerned.

The principal aims of the Patent Cooperation Treaty are to save time, work, and money for both the applicants and the patent offices and to increase the likelihood of issuing strong patents in countries that lack facilities for thorough search and examination. The treaty promises relief from the multiple filing burden by providing a central filing, search, and examination system for the Paris Union countries adhering to it. The joint congressional resolution adopted in 1969 recited these reasons for the adoption of such a treaty:

All countries issuing patents, and especially countries such as the United States having an examination system, deal with large and growing numbers of patent applications of increasing complexity. In any one country a considerable number of patent applications duplicate, or substantially duplicate, applications relating to the same inventions in other countries, thereby increasing further the volume of applications to be processed. A resolution of the difficulties attendant upon duplications in filings and examination would result in more economical, quicker, and more effective protection for inventions throughout the world, thus benefiting inventors, the general public, and governments.

At the conclusion of the conference, delegates from twenty countries, including the United States, the United Kingdom, West Germany, Italy, and Japan, signed the treaty provisionally. Spokesmen for other countries voiced approval but explained that they were required to consult their governments before affixing their signatures to the document. The U.S. delegation announced that Senate approval would be necessary and that the U.S. patent law would have to be amended to authorize, among other things, acceptance of the projected international application. One point had been ironed out at the conference: the United States would be permitted to retain for "prior art" purposes the filing date in this country rather than the filing date in a foreign country of origin, which makes amendment of the American law in this respect unnecessary.

The treaty was to remain open for signature until the end of 1970 and was to enter into force three months after ratification by eight nations, at least four of which must have major patent activity. Provisions had been added to the treaty that were calculated to aid developing nations by furnishing them

Left to right: Dr. William Thomas Green Morton, James Bogardus, Samuel Colt, Cyrus Hall McCormick, Joseph Saxton, Charles Goodyear (seated), Peter Cooper (pointing), Jordan Lawrence Mott (seated), Professor Joseph Henry (standing), Dr. Eliphalet Nott, John Ericsson, Frederick Ellsworth Sickels, Samuel Finley Breese Morse, Henry Burden, Richard March Hoe, Erastus Brigham Bigelow, Isaiah Jennings, Thomas Blanchard, Elias Howe.

Men of Progress, a group portrait of famous nineteenth-century inventors, painted by Christian Schussele (1826–79). Applications for many early patents were accom-panied by three-dimensional models like those on the floor and the table. (*National Portrait Gallery, Smithsonian Institution, Washington, D.C.*)

The old Patent Office on Northwest F Street, Washington. The building is now occupied by the Smithsonian Institution's National Collection of Fine Arts and National Portrait Gallery.

Two of the three eleven-story buildings housing the modern Patent Office at Crystal Plaza, Arlington County, Virginia. The Search Room occupies the two-story annex connecting the two buildings.

General view of the Patent Office Search Room at Crystal Plaza.

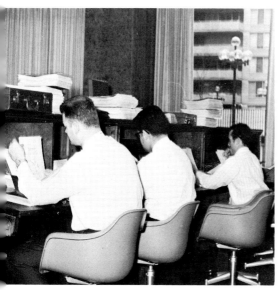

Above: Searchers work at desks in the modern Search Room. *Right*: A searcher thumbs through a bundle of "hard" (cardboard) copies of patents.

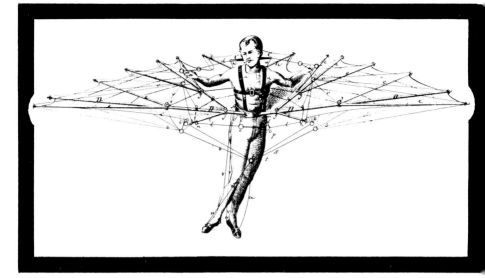

Human flight has inspired many inventors. Here are two patents pertaining to flight—one invention that worked and one that did not.

Above: The Flying Apparatus patented in 1872 by Watson F. Quinby of Wilmington, Delaware, which relied on flapping wings. *Below:* The Flying Machine invented by Orville and Wilbur Wright of Dayton, Ohio, and patented in 1906, three years after their first successful powered flight.

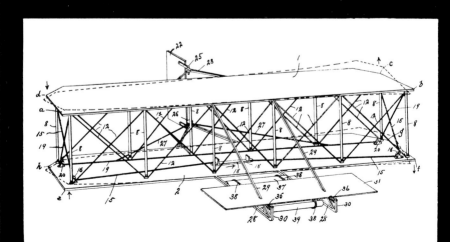

Leonardo da Vinci (1452–1519) designed several devices for propelling or parachuting man through the air. Here are three models constructed from drawings in Leonardo's notebooks by the International Business Machines Corporation and displayed at the Patent Office and at museums and universities throughout the United States.

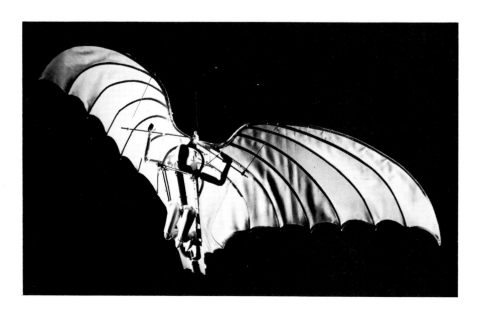

SOME LANDMARK PATENTS

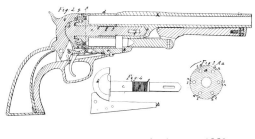

Samuel Colt: six-shooter, 1850.

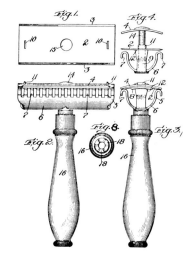

King C. Gillette:
safety razor, 1904.

Whitcomb L. Judson:
the first zipper, 1893.

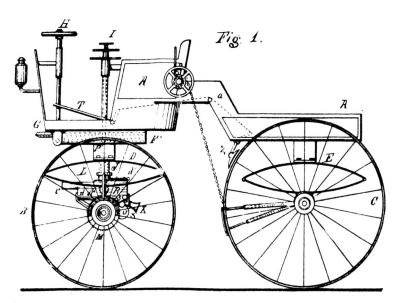

George B. Selden: Road Engine, 1895. The story of this controversial patent, which was successfully challenged by Henry Ford, is told in Chapter IV.

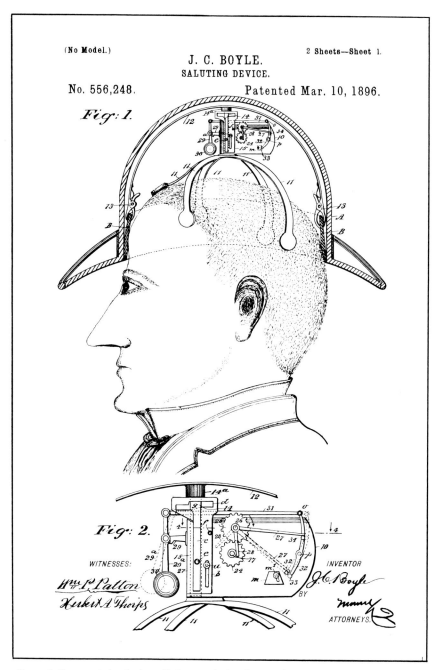

One of the most intriguing, if impractical, nineteenth-century inventions was the Saluting Device patented in 1896 by James C. Boyle of Spokane, Washington. This self-tipping hat enabled its wearer to salute a lady by merely nodding, even though his arms were full of packages.

Onward and upward (and sometimes downward) with some examples of nineteenth-century patent art—

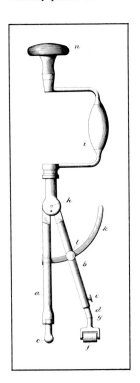

Above: Hunting Decoy, patented in 1897 by John Sievers, Jr., of Ames, Nebraska.

Left: Device for Producing Dimples, patented in 1896 by Martin Goetze of Berlin, Germany.

Below: Fire-Escape, patented in 1879 by Benjamin B. Oppenheimer of Trenton, Tennessee.

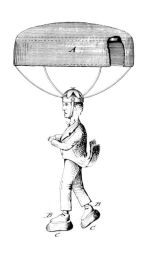

information on patents and published applications, and a Committee for Technical Assistance was authorized to help such nations by training specialists, lending experts, and supplying equipment.

Under the treaty the procedure for American inventors will be about as follows:

In a typical case, within twelve months after filing his regular U.S. application, the applicant will file an international application in the U.S. Patent Office, designating the member countries in which he seeks patent protection for the same invention. The international application will be in English but will serve as a complete application and will be entitled to the same filing date in each of the designated countries. The U.S. Patent Office will keep a copy of the international application, and by the end of the thirteenth month will send another to the secretariat (BIRPI*) in Geneva as record copy.

In the next three months the U.S. Patent Office will conduct an extensive international search, listing in a report the relevant prior patents and publications it finds. One copy of the report will go to the applicant and another to BIRPI. Basing his decision on this search report, the applicant can let his international application stand, withdraw it, or amend the claims, within the next two months through BIRPI.

By the end of the eighteenth month after filing, BIRPI will send copies of the application, any amendments, and the search report to each designated country. By the end of the twentieth month, the applicant will owe national filing fees to the countries designated, and he must send a translation of his application to each country in which the national language is not English. This means he has gained eight months—over the twelve provided in the Convention of Paris—in which

* BIRPI is an acronym for the French name of the secretariat, rendered into English as United International Bureaux for the Protection of Intellectual Property. ("Intellectual" indicates the inclusion of copyrights as well as patents and trademarks.)

to make up his mind whether going further is worth the expense.

An optional feature of the treaty program may give the applicant an extra five months, or a total of twenty-five, to make up his mind. This involves his decision, to be exercised by the end of the nineteenth month, on whether to apply for an international preliminary examination report in those member countries that have adhered to Chapter 2 of the treaty. (A country may adhere to Chapter 2 with the reservation that its patent office need not postpone national publication for the full twenty-five months.)

If the international *search* report turns out to be unfavorable, the applicant may want to ask the U.S. Patent Office for the preliminary *examination* report, indicating whether each claim is likely to be granted. Copies will go to the chosen countries by way of BIRPI.

WORLD INTELLECTUAL PROPERTY ORGANIZATION

To improve the administration of the projected Patent Cooperation Treaty and other international agreements, a strengthened secretariat has been proposed to succeed BIRPI. A convention establishing the World Intellectual Property Organization (WIPO) was signed on behalf of the United States and other countries at Stockholm on July 14, 1967. In March, 1969, President Richard M. Nixon sent the convention to the Senate for consent to its ratification, saying that WIPO would provide a coordinated administration for the various intellectual property unions managed by BIRPI and would advance protection generally on a worldwide basis. By that time the number of signatory governments had reached fifty-one.

In the same message the President asked the Senate to consent to revision of the original Paris Convention so as to modernize the Paris Union it had created. The revised convention had been signed by representatives of the United States and many other countries at the Stockholm meeting in 1967. Under the revision, the member governments relieve the Swiss government of responsibilities in supervision of the secretariat and other matters.

One amendment, which was regarded as improving relations with Eastern European countries, would grant the same priority rights (as to recognition of filing dates) on inventors' certificates as on patents. A proviso was added that the Eastern European countries concerned would maintain a dual system of patents and inventors' certificates and make both available to applicants. A bill was introduced in the U.S. Senate in June, 1970, to amend the patent law so as to accomplish such recognition of inventors' certificates. An inventor's certificate does not, as a patent does, give the inventor an exclusive right to his invention. Instead, the application may be considered an offer of the invention to the government. The inventor, in return, is entitled to an award depending on the economic value of his concept. Generally, the inventor applies for the certificate, but in the Soviet Union, if he has developed the idea as part of his job, the agency employing him may file.

A report to the White House by William P. Rogers, Secretary of State, which was forwarded to the Senate, said in part:

In the 1960's there has been much ferment and change in the industrial and copyright fields. Some of the changes have advanced protection; changes in certain countries have reduced the level of protection. The new W.I.P.O. will be better prepared to cope with the rapidly moving developments concerning industrial property and copyright protection occurring all over the world. Administratively it will be a more efficient organization. Substantively it will provide a forum to which industrialized as well as developing countries may bring intellectual property problems for consideration by technical experts assisted by a technically competent secretariat in an atmosphere conducive to reasoned and objective discussions. It is highly desirable for the United States as the country with the most valuable foreign industrial property and copyright interests in the world to move ahead expeditiously toward membership in [WIPO] the only international organization devoted exclusively to intellectual property protection.

Mr. Rogers cited support for WIPO and the amendment of the Paris Convention by the American Bar Association's Patent, Trademark, and Copyright Law Section, the American Patent Law Association, and other American bar and business organizations, and the Senate, in 1970, gave its consent both on WIPO and on the Paris Convention revision.

The International Bureau, successor of the present secretariat, BIRPI, is to administer one international agreement concerning copyrights and six relating to industrial property (such as patents and trademarks). The United States is a party only to the Paris Convention.

The convention relating to copyrights is formally known as the Berne Convention of September 9, 1886, for the Protection of Literary and Artistic Works. Although the United States has not adhered to it, some American publishers have in the past taken advantage of its provisions in countries not subscribing to the Universal Copyright Convention, to which the United States *is* a party. The latter convention was ratified by the United States November 5, 1954, and became effective in this country September 16, 1955. Through this arrangement, more than fifty countries (not including the Soviet Union) give American copyright registrants the same protection that they accord their own nationals.

The five industrial property arrangements to which certain other member countries, but not the United States, adhere are known formally as: the Madrid Agreement of April 14, 1891, for the Repression of False or Deceptive Indications of Source on Goods; the Madrid Agreement of April 14, 1891, concerning the International Registration of Marks; the Hague Agreement of November 6, 1925, concerning the International

Deposit of Industrial Designs; the Nice Agreement of June 15, 1957, concerning the International Classification of Goods and Services for the Purposes of Registration of Marks; and the Lisbon Agreement of October 31, 1958, for the Protection of Appellations of Origin and Their International Registration. The United States has considered adhering to the second of these agreements—the Madrid Agreement on the International Registration of Marks—or to a comparable agreement yet to be negotiated (see "International Trademark Registration," below).

INTERNATIONAL ACTIVITIES OF THE U.S. PATENT OFFICE

An Office of International Patent and Trademark Affairs, set up in the U.S. Patent Office in 1964, has carried on joint studies with a number of foreign patent offices. One reason for the formation of this unit was that most of the initiative for international cooperation in the period after World War II had come from abroad, and there was a feeling that the United States should take a position of leadership.

Lists of references cited during the searches of patent applications have been exchanged with the patent offices of West Germany, the United Kingdom, France, Switzerland, Sweden, Czechoslovakia, Austria, Japan, and some other nations. Under a professional training program, examiners have been exchanged with West Germany, Japan, Canada, the United Kingdom, the Netherlands, and the International Patent Institute maintained at The Hague by various foreign governments.

For several years the Office of International Patent and Trademark Affairs has had a member of its staff on duty at the office of BIRPI in Geneva. Part of his work involves the activities of ICIREPAT (International Cooperation in Information Retrieval Among Examining Patent Offices), a technical committee, originally formed for cooperation in mechanized searching. The group has extended its work to all aspects of documentation, including microforms. The U.S. Patent Office uses international classification symbols, in addition to its own, on U.S. patents and trademarks. Another sign of international cooperation is the Patent Office's exchange of patent copies with many countries. A 1969 tabulation showed current receipt of patents from Australia, Austria, Belgium, Canada, Czechoslovakia, Denmark, East Germany, Egypt, Finland, France, Germany, Great Britain, India, Ireland, Italy, Japan, Korea, the Netherlands, Norway, Poland, Romania, Sweden, Switzerland, and the Soviet Union.

Over the last five years, the number of patent applications filed by Americans abroad has steadily increased, and so has the number filed in this country by foreign inventors. Indeed, these foreign applicants have been the chief cause of the increased work load in the U.S. Patent Office. Both in this country and abroad, the number of inventions being patented has remained virtually constant, but protection for them is being sought in an increasing number of countries.

COMMON PATENTS, COMMON PROCEDURE

A single patent, valid in all six countries of the common market, and a unified European system of obtaining patents are approaching reality. A common market patent for all members of the European Economic Community—Belgium, France, Italy, Luxembourg, the Netherlands, and Germany—had been projected in the early 1960's but the scheme lay dormant until the idea, and its extension, were revived early in 1969. At conferences held in the spring of that year, seven additional countries that had shown interest in the idea were invited to participate. These were Ireland, Great Britain, Norway, Denmark, Sweden, Austria, and Switzerland. Spain, Greece, Turkey, Portugal, and Monaco were also represented, making a total of eighteen. Two conventions were planned.

Under one, the six common market countries would harmonize their patent laws and create a single patent valid in all. The other convention would open to other countries the system of obtaining patents—by one application to a central office, one search, and one examining procedure.

In the discussions there were references to a "European patent." However, national patents would result. Dr. Kurt Haertel, president of the German patent office and one of the architects of the plan, explained the matter to an American audience in these words: "The European patent shall be so designed as to disintegrate, upon being granted, into a group of national patents whose legal effects depend exclusively on the national law of the member state concerned." Under the proposal, applications would be examined for novelty, with a search report made by the International Patent Institute at The Hague. Examination would be deferred unless the applicant made a demand for it when he filed. Deferred examination systems, such as that in the Netherlands, relieve the patent offices of the burden of passing on all applications and allow an inventor to drop a case if he prefers.

It was not clear whether American inventors could take advantage of the European patent procedure. It was announced that outside countries could participate if they granted the same protection to the nationals of the signatory states as they gave their own citizens when granting them national patents. United States laws differ from those abroad, particularly as to priority of invention.

At a Brussels meeting in May, 1969, a committee of experts from Great Britain, Sweden, Switzerland, the Netherlands, Germany, and France was appointed, with Dr. Haertel as chairman, to draft an agreement for the European patent system to be submitted to a general meeting later. A Nordic patent system is also pending at this writing. Under the agreement signed in 1963 on behalf of Denmark, Finland, Norway, and Sweden, each of the four patent offices would grant separate national patents, but at an inventor's request his application would also be forwarded to any of the others he designated. Operation was delayed pending harmonization of the patent laws.

A single patent for all thirteen countries of the African and Malagasy Union, former French colonies, can be obtained through the African and Malagasy Industrial Property Office in Yaoundé, Cameroun. The term is twenty years. It is, however, a "registration" patent, not examined for novelty. Disputes are settled through the courts of the member countries.

JOINT U.S.–PHILIPPINES PROGRAM

A U.S. cooperative arrangement with the Philippines, inaugurated in 1968, is designed to save time and expense for patent applicants who want to protect an invention in both countries. An American inventor, for instance, who files in the United States and subsequently applies in the Philippines sends with the latter application a notice in duplicate that he has elected to follow the special procedure. The notice certifies that the description, claims, and drawings are identical with those filed in the U.S. Patent Office, and the signer agrees to supply the same amendments if any are made here.

The Philippines Patent Office sends the U.S. Patent Office one copy of the notice of election it has received and defers action until it receives information on disposal of the U.S. application. The Philippines office then makes its decision; if it wishes, it may ask the applicant to show cause why the results of the U.S. examination should not be accepted in the Philippines. In the case of an application first filed in the Philippines, a similar procedure is followed.

Like the United States and Canada, the Republic of the Philippines recognizes the inventor who was first to invent, not the first to file.

INTERNATIONAL TRADEMARK REGISTRATION

For several years, American interests have studied the value of adherence by the United States to the Madrid Agreement of April 14, 1891, concerning the International Registration of Marks. Under this agreement, the owner registers a trademark or service mark in the member country where he lives. He then files a single international application with BIRPI, the Geneva secretariat, in one language (French) and pays a single fee, instead of filing separately in the national offices, in different languages, and paying a separate fee in each. The registration can be similarly renewed every tenth or twentieth year.

Every registration is effective in several countries, potentially in all the member states of the Madrid Union (in 1969 there were twenty-one). The international registration is published by BIRPI and sent to the member states in which the applicant seeks protection. Unless a state refuses within one year, the international registration becomes effective as a national registration. BIRPI reports that refusals are rare in countries whose national laws do not provide for examination of applications, and this is true of more than half of the members.

To qualify, an applicant must be a national of one of the member states, or must be domiciled or have a real and effective industrial or commercial establishment in one of them. Chief advantages for Americans accruing from adherence to the agreement would be avoidance of the complexity and high cost of filing trademark applications in a large number of separate jurisdictions. At present, to protect an American mark around the world, this means about 150 separate filings, widely varying in requirements, term, language, and fees. Exclusive of searches, lawyers' time, and other expenses, the cost has been estimated at from $125 to $150 per application, or a total of from $18,750 to $22,500 per mark.

A committee of businessmen studied the problem for the Secretary of Commerce in 1967 but did not render a formal report. The United States Trademark Association, the American Patent Law Association, the Patent, Trademark, and Copyright Law Section of the American Bar Association, and the American Group of the International Patent and Trademark Association have arrived at generally the same basic conclusions: that the United States should continue to work toward participation in a system of international registration of marks but that we should not adhere to the Madrid agreement as it now stands. The feeling is that the membership should be larger and that participation of certain countries that do not now belong would be important. These include Japan, the United Kingdom, and the Scandinavian countries.

The United States sent a delegation to a meeting of experts, held in Geneva, April 13 to 16, 1970, to consider revision of the Madrid Agreement of 1891 so as to meet objections of nonparticipants. Twenty-two countries were represented. The reluctance of many of the member countries to alter key provisions of the existing agreement proved disappointing to the Americans. The U.S. delegation recommended the convening of a wider assembly, which could bring together all members of the Paris Union and work toward a universal system of trademark registration.

WORLD PATENT INDEX

An international service called the World Patent Index has been proposed by BIRPI, the secretariat in Geneva, and the International Patent Institute, which is maintained at The Hague by various member governments, not including the United States, as a technical documentation search center for industry as well as governments. The World Patent Index would report from an office in Europe what was being patented, in what fields, by whom, and where. It would spot multiple patents for the same invention in any of eighty countries.

When the plan was first proposed in 1966, the U.S. Patent Office gave it a friendly reception and explained the proposed procedure at meetings in various cities. It was said that the World Patent Index would make it possible for interested persons to identify "families" of patents and published patent applications based on the same priority claim (filing date in the home country) under the Paris Convention. A standing order could be placed, renewable from year to year, so that, with reference to an identified patent or application in a given country, the subscriber would be automatically notified of the filing of another application or the granting of another patent for the same invention as soon as the filing or grant was published. In the United States, applications are kept secret pending the issuance of patents. In many countries they are made public.

In its proposal for a World Patent Index, BIRPI estimated that in the ten years 1967–76 about 650,000 patent applications would be filed annually in 80 national patent offices, and about 320,000 patents relating to some 100,000 different inventions would be issued each year. This means that in this 10-year period the World Patent Index would deal with 3.2 million patents covering a million different inventions—a volume that would require computer operation.

At this writing, the sponsors still favor establishment of the World Patent Index, but it has not yet gotten under way.

LOCARNO AGREEMENT ON INDUSTRIAL DESIGNS

An agreement setting up an international classification for industrial designs was signed by representatives of the United States and twenty-one other governments (including the Holy See) at a diplomatic conference in Locarno, Switzerland, on October 8, 1968. A committee of experts, including American representatives, was established by the agreement, to compile a manual of industrial designs, arranged alphabetically, or with an index, and to make necessary corrections in the tentative classifications.

Thirty-one main classes and more than two hundred subclasses were listed in the agreement. The main classes include (under more specific titles) foods, clothing, travel goods, brushes, textiles, furniture, household goods, hardware, packages, clocks, jewelry, vehicles, electrical equipment, machinery, cameras, and musical instruments. Other classes involve office machines, stationery, sales and vending devices, toys, arms and hunting equipment, sanitary fittings, medical equipment, building units, lighting apparatus, tobacco, pharmaceuticals and cosmetics, and safety devices for man and beast.

In the United States, industrial designs are protected by design patents, granted for three and a half, seven, or fourteen years. Most other governments have systems for protection of industrial designs by registration, without examination, and not necessarily by patents. U.S. design patents are marked with both the United States and international classifications. As an example, take Design Patent 214,010, granted to Arthur Carew of Sausalito, California, in 1969 for a fur-trimmed coat. The abbreviation on the printed patent, Int. Cl. D2—*01* means that it belongs in Class 2 (Articles of Clothing, Including Footwear) under Subclass 01 (Garments).

Secretariat work is performed by BIRPI, which administers the agreement. U.S. patent officials regard use of the international classification as helpful to examiners and attorneys in searching the records, particularly abroad, for prior design patents and publications.

PATENTS IN DEVELOPING COUNTRIES

The importance of patent systems to the progress of underdeveloped countries was recognized years ago by BIRPI, the secretariat at Geneva, by a group of experts who met at its invitation, and by the United Nations. In 1964, the United Nations published a hundred-page study, *The Role of Patents in the Transfer of Technology to Developing Countries*. G. H. C. Bodenhausen, director of BIRPI, discussed the matter at a conference on world patent systems, held in New York in 1965 under the sponsorship of the National Association of Manufacturers:

> One of the prerequisites of the development of these nations is rapid industrialization. For this, they need to assimilate and use to the maximum extent foreign investment, foreign inventions, and foreign technical know-how. Adequate protection of these elements will naturally encourage the licensing, for local production, of foreign inventions and know-how, and will attract foreign investment. It will also encourage local inventive talent, as demonstrated by the experience of highly developed countries.

After consultations with the representatives of African, Asian, and Latin nations and other members of the Paris Union, as well as observers from the United Nations and various associations, BIRPI prepared and proceeded to publish in several languages its *Model Law for Developing Countries on Inventions*. Four newly independent African countries were already considering the draft in preparing patent legislation. The model law was offered, not as something that must be followed exactly, but as an adaptable framework. The requirements of patentability included provisions that the invention was new, that it resulted from inventive activity, and was capable of industrial application. Exceptions from patentability were plant and animal varieties, the biological processes necessary to their production, and inventions contrary to public order or morality. Priority was to go to the first to file. The term of a patent was to be twenty years, subject to the payment of required annual fees.

Under the model law, three alternatives were offered with regard to examination: a "registration" system without examination; an examination system like that in the United States; and a system of deferred examination like that offered in the Netherlands and Germany. In the realization that a developing country might be short of trained technical personnel and have difficulty in organizing an examining corps, the draft included provisions for use of search results obtained from the International Patent Institute at The Hague or from national patent offices. Since most patentees in a developing country may be foreigners, the model law included sections on the regulation of licenses, with compulsory licensing in such cases as a lapse of four years without the invention being worked or refusal of the owner to grant licenses on reasonable terms.

The model law also contained provisions for the protection of technical know-how. Annexes covered possible coverage of "patents of introduction" and inventors' certificates such as granted in the Soviet Union and other socialist countries of Eastern Europe. A patent of introduction was defined as one of relatively short duration (for example, ten years). It is granted in the expectation that the patentee, who is also the owner of the foreign patent, will exploit the invention in the developing country. Importation of the invention is prohibited, and the patent of introduction may become void if exploitation does not start within two years.

A model law for developing countries on marks, trade names, and acts of unfair competition was similarly developed by BIRPI and published in 1967, and a model law on designs was scheduled for publication.

Quite aside from patents, one effort to aid developing countries has met with objections from the United States. This involved action at the intellectual property conference held in Stockholm in 1967 concerning the Berne Convention of 1886 for the Protection of Literary and Artistic Works. The United States, which adheres to the Universal Copyright Convention, was also considering adherence to the Berne Convention, but a "protocol regarding developing countries," adopted at Stockholm, changed the State Department's mind. Eugene M. Braderman, chairman of the U.S. delegation, said in a formal report that the protocol "has made it virtually impossible for the United States to consider Berne adherence within the foreseeable future."

THE INTERNATIONAL TREND

As world trade expands, protecting inventions is no longer a domestic matter. Officials and businessmen are tired of doing the same thing twenty times in twenty different ways. Officials and attorneys might deny that their burdens were actually becoming lighter, but both the government agencies involved and the patent departments of corporations are finding it easier to cope with the increasing volume and complexity of their work. The red tape on industrial property is getting a little looser.

Practices in many countries on such matters as the classification of inventions and marks are more nearly uniform. Although the laws are all different, men on opposite sides of international borders are coming to think more alike. A universal patent, valid throughout the world, still remains a dream. But it soon should be possible to get patents on the same invention in many jurisdictions with one application, one search, and one examination. And the common market hopes before long to launch a single patent good in all six countries.

VI

If Not a Patent, What?

As a guardian of inventions, the patent system has no real rival. However, several alternatives are open to an inventor. To avoid getting a patent, an inventor can try to keep his discovery secret. He may choose the trade secret route—or he can do the reverse and give his discovery to the public, as Dr. Jonas Salk did with his vaccine for poliomyelitis. Scientists to whom prestige is valuable but who consider it unethical to seek patent rights can take due credit but eschew royalties by disclosing their achievements in professional journals.

The trade secret route is open to the man who wants to profit but does not choose to patent or copyright. Trade secrets are older than patents. In the Fall 1966 issue of its journal *IDEA,* the PTC (Patent, Trademark, and Copyright) Research Institute of George Washington University pointed out that the patent system replaced the guild system of the Middle Ages. Under the guild codes, an innovation remained secret indefinitely, and in certain instances the technology died with the last members of the guild. The patent system discloses the trade secret to the public in return for a monopoly right over a limited period.

The growing reliance on trade secrets in recent years is sometimes attributed to the time lag in processing patent applications. The PTC Institute has termed a much more important factor the vast increase in industrial activity, which generates inventions, whatever their quality, at an unprecedented rate. A company using an invention more than a year before applying for a patent may be able to depend only on secrecy for protection. And there is always the temptation to test the market before patenting.

Studies by the Institute have indicated that many assigned and unassigned inventions are first tried in the market place, and only those that are commercially viable are patented. Statistics suggest that in an average year there may be anywhere between 30,000 and 60,000 patentable inventions for which no application is filed.

Sometimes a concern decides to forget about a patent and to put a product on the market so fast that the competition can't catch up. One patent lawyer comments: "I have given such advice at times to an inventor or small company where the item was ephemeral, such as a toy, game, or gadget that would have a short market life and where patentability is questionable. In such case I suggest that a manufactured inventory be built up of the item and that distribution to the best volume outlets be effected in as short a time as possible before competitors can get started." A patent application can still be filed within one year of the first sale if the demand justifies such action.

Trade secrets, of course, constitute a much broader field than patentable inventions because they include know-how—the technical instructions whose use can be licensed. The licensing of trade secrets and know-how has, however, been challenged by certain members of the Supreme Court in a recent case (*Lear* v. *Adkins*).

Employment agreements with inventors usually include restrictions on the disclosure of trade secrets either during or after employment and require the return of records and drawings to the company after the job is ended. An authority on the legal aspects of the trade secret problem is quoted in Appendix D.

If a company's only interest is to assure its own right to use an invention, it may choose defensive patenting and grant licenses freely. Or it may choose the simpler method of defensive publication, which is cheaper than patenting. By openly printing the details of his invention, an inventor prevents any other inventor from getting a patent on the concept unless the other inventor can prove invention prior to the disclosure. The defensive publication program of the Patent Office has already been described in Chapter III. International Business Machines Corporation publishes its own monthly *IBM Technical Disclosure Bulletin* for concepts originating in its laboratories.

Even after an application has been filed, disclosure can still be made. Under the heading "Defensive Publications," the weekly *Official Gazette* of the Patent Office prints abstracts and drawings of applications listed by serial number. These notices are inserted at the request of the applicants or assignees. If the information given in an abstract is insufficient, the public can go to the files or get a copy of the application, including drawings and claims, upon payment of a nominal charge per sheet. The applications have not been examined, and the Patent Office makes no assertion as to novelty.

It is also possible to surrender part of a patent or part of its term. A patent owner may publish a notice in the *Official Gazette* that he "hereby enters this disclaimer to claim 3 of said patent." This may mean that the claim has been held invalid by a court. If the owner maintains an action for a valid claim in the patent before disclaiming an invalid claim, he cannot recover costs of the suit.

A terminal disclaimer may recite that the inventor or his assignee "hereby disclaims the terminal portion of the term of the patent" subsequent to some specified date. In such a case the owner probably holds two patents in the same general field and wishes both to expire with the term of the earlier one. He is clipping off the end of the second patent to avoid a question as to whether it covers a patentable invention separate and distinct from that covered in the first patent. An invention is entitled to only one seventeen-year patent, and the law discourages "double patenting."

It is worth noting that the President's Commission on the Patent System, in its 1966 report, recommended that all provisions in the patent law for design patents and plant patents be eliminated and that some other means of protection be provided. The commission also urged that computer programs, regardless of form, not be considered patentable.

COPYRIGHTING DESIGNS

A good many designs are copyrighted rather than patented, because the process is relatively simple and quick—taking about three weeks as compared to an average of about a year for design patents. Speed may be an advantage with products of short commercial life. However, the requirement that the design must be a work of art under the copyright law and the fact that protection is limited to copying should be kept in mind when copyright rather than patent protection is considered.

Designs fall in four graphic art categories, which are officially described as follows:

Works of art; or models or designs for works of art (Class G). Published or unpublished works of artistic craftsmanship, insofar as their form but not their mechanical or utilitarian aspects are concerned, such as artistic jewelry, enamels, glassware, and tapestries, as well as works belonging to the fine arts, such as paintings, drawings, and sculpture.

Reproductions of works of art (Class H). Published reproductions of existing works of art in the same or a different medium, such as a lithograph, photoengraving, etching, or drawing of a painting, sculpture, or other work of art.

Drawings or sculptured works of a scientific or technical character (Class I). Published or unpublished diagrams or models illustrating scientific or technical works, such as an architect's or engineer's blueprint, plan, or design, a mechanical drawing, an astronomical chart, or an anatomical model.

Prints, pictorial illustrations, and commercial prints or labels (Class K). Published prints or pictorial illustrations, greeting cards, picture postcards, and similar prints, produced by means of lithography, photoengraving, or other methods of reproduction. A print or label, not a trademark, published in connection with the sale or advertisement of articles of merchandise also is registered in this class.

In fiscal year 1969, there were 16,306 registrations in the four graphic arts classes. For an unpublished work—that is, one of which copies have not been sold, offered for sale, or otherwise made available to the public—an application form and one copy of the work are filed. For a published work, the application form and two copies or photographs of the work bearing the copyright notice in prescribed form are required. The registration fee is $6.

Application forms and general information are obtainable by mail from the Register of Copyrights, Library of Congress, Washington, D.C., 20540. All mail should be so addressed, but present quarters are actually in Crystal Mall, 1921 Jefferson Davis Highway, Arlington, Virginia, near the Patent Office.

The owner of a copyright has the right to prevent all others from copying the work without his permission. A work is not disqualified from protection as a "work of art" solely because it is embodied in a functional article. Courts have held that jewelry, dolls, artificial flowers, and textile fabrics are copyrightable. But the Register of Copyrights, on the basis of court decisions, has reported that "copyright in a pictorial, graphic, or sculptural work, portraying a useful article as such, does not extend to the manufacture of the useful article itself." Thus a copyright in a drawing or model of an automobile does not give the artist the exclusive right to make automobiles of the same mechanical construction. For several years hearings and discussions have been held on general revision of the copyright law. The latest of a number of bills (which passed the House in 1967 and was introduced in the Senate in 1969) appears not to make essential alterations in the coverage of designs. One general change, although of little interest to design owners, is to extend duration of copyright from twenty-eight years plus a renewal for twenty-eight years to the life of the author and fifty years after his death.

REGISTRATION OF DESIGNS

For more than a decade, a group of businessmen has sought legislation to provide better protection against design piracy. Organized as the National Committee for Effective Design Legislation, with headquarters in New York, the group has promoted a succession of bills, three of which have passed the Senate but not the House. The committee, whose counsel is Alan Latman, a New York lawyer, has defined design piracy as the unauthorized copying of the appearance of someone else's product—the appropriation of artistic work that is commercially valuable to its creator. The pirate relies on the commercial success of another's venture.

Piracy is regarded as harmful to designers, manufacturers, distributors, retailers, suppliers, and consumers. Better legal protection would, it is said, relieve designers of the degrading, wasteful, and troublesome practices forced upon them by widespread piracy. In some industries, designers consciously try to produce a design difficult to copy. One originator of men's sport shirts offered a "mystery shirt," sight unseen, because of his certainty that his design would be destroyed by copying as soon as it was revealed.

The committee has set forth in these words why the present laws do not provide effective protection:

Patents are too difficult to obtain, too slow and too expensive. Basically, there are two types of patents. The type usually thought of when one hears the word "patent" is a mechanical patent, a grant by the U.S. Government protecting the functional operation of a machine, manufacture or process. In addition, there are patents protecting appearance. The latter are called design patents and differ from mechanical patents only with respect to length of protection (the term for mechanical patents is seventeen years while design patents last for three and a half, seven or fourteen years, depending on whether the applicant chooses to pay a fee of ten, twenty or thirty dollars).

In order to qualify for a patent, an applicant must introduce something new to a particular field. But he must do more than merely take a step forward—it must be a large step. The contribution must be such that it was not "obvious" to those in the field. These requirements are what patent lawyers mean when they speak of "novelty" and "invention."

It is apparent that many attractive and successful designs in such fields as wearing apparel, kitchen-ware, automobiles and furniture fail to meet these high standards. The results in the Patent Office and the courts have convinced designers and manufacturers that design patents are difficult to obtain and difficult to enforce. And even if the requirements were not so high, it is apparent that judgments about appearance must be highly objective and unpredictable.

In view of the requirement that a design be novel, a search of earlier designs must be conducted by the Patent Office before it can issue a patent. Until the patent is actually granted, the designer or manufacturer markets his design at his peril. The time lag, which can be many months, is thus crucial.

Finally, the overall expense of design patents is much greater than the statutory fees mentioned above. Even such fees must be multiplied by the number of designs introduced by a manufacturer each year. But in addition, a manufacturer who decides to rely on a patent must usually first seek the advice of patent counsel. Thus the cost of a preliminary search and legal fees also add to the expenses of securing a design patent.

Copyright protection for "works of art" covers only relatively few designs, and even those covered receive a type of protection which does not fit the situation.

A copyright is not as difficult to obtain as a patent. The author need only originate the work himself, that is, refrain from copying from someone else's work or from the common fund of works known as the "public domain." And he can obtain a copyright not only for a book, play or musical composition, but also for a "work of art."

Can the design of a useful article be considered a "work of art" as that term is used in the copyright statute? This is a question which has been troubling the courts and the U.S. Copyright Office for some time. The answer is that sometimes such designs have been considered "works of art", but more often they have not.

Neither the courts nor the Copyright Office set themselves up as art critics. In fact, the function of the latter is much more restricted than that of the Patent Office. The Copyright Office merely examines claims to copyright to determine whether the work seems to fall within the subject matter which Congress has said is copyrightable; it does not search, for example, to see whether the same work has been created by someone earlier or whether something offered as a "work of art" is a particularly good work of art. Nevertheless, this Office, as well as the courts in infringement suits, must decide whether Congress intended the particular work in question to be included within the protection of the copyright law.

Beginning in 1957, legislation to provide design protection has been offered in each Congress. Bills passed the Senate in 1962, 1964, and 1966, but not the House. Identical measures introduced in the Senate and House in the 91st Congress were entitled Design Protection Act of 1969. The provisions were also incorporated as Title III of S.543, the copyright law revision bill, which failed to pass the Senate in 1970.

The proposed act offers protection for original ornamental designs of useful articles for five years, with a renewal for the same period. Applications are to be examined only as to whether the design is on its face registrable—that is, whether it meets the statutory requirements for protection—but there are no references to "prior art" or search to establish novelty, lack of obviousness, or inventiveness. An administrator is to handle the registrations, but the agency is not designated. The bill says merely, "The Administrator and Office of the Administrator referred to in this Act shall be such officer and office as the President may designate." In some of the hearings, the Patent Office was mentioned as the agency to have charge.

Protection is to be afforded the author or other proprietor of an original ornamental design of a useful article. A "useful article" is defined as an article which in normal use has an intrinsic utilitarian function that is not merely to portray the appearance of the article or to convey information. The "design of a useful article" consists of those aspects or elements, including its two-dimensional or three-dimensional features of shape and surface that make up the appearance of the article. A design is "ornamental" if it is intended to make the article attractive or distinctive in appearance. A design is "original" if it is the independent creation of an author who did not copy it from another source.

Among articles excepted from coverage are those "composed of three-dimensional features of shape and surface with respect to men's, women's and children's apparel including undergarments and outerwear." Protection for clothing was eliminated, it is understood, because of objections voiced by retailers and apparel manufacturers at hearings on previous bills.

Applications for registration must be filed within six months of the date the design (as embodied in an actual article) was first made public and must be accompanied by two copies of a drawing or other pictorial representation. Related useful articles may be included in the same application. When granted, registrations are to be published. They are subject to cancellation if anyone can satisfy the administrator that the person has been or will be damaged and the design should not have been registered. Filing fees are $15, with $10 more for each additional related article to be included. Products are to be marked with the words "Protected Design" or an abbreviation.

In infringement, the owner of a registered design is to have remedy by civil action, and injunctions may be granted. Courts may allow damages to $5,000, or $1 per copy, and may grant higher awards if such action appears just in the circumstances. The proposed law would terminate its protection once the article has been covered by a design patent. An amendment to the copyright law included in the same bills would terminate any existing copyright protection, to the extent the protection applies to a useful article, once the article is registered under the design protection act.

What are the chances for the passage of such a design protection law? The attitude of the bar associations has been generally favorable. In its 1966 report, the President's Commission on the Patent System recommended that design patents be eliminated and that some means of protection outside the patent system be developed. The Patent Office has indicated that it has the subject under study, but observers have been cautious in predicting action on the pending bills.

PROTECTING SOFTWARE

The developers of computer programs have been dissatisfied with patent protection for their wares as indicated in the account of the software controversy in Chapter X. Nor is the growing software industry generally content to rely on copyrights, or a combination of copyrights and trade secrecy. One procedure sometimes adopted has been to place a copyright notice on the printed part of a program and to lease the accompanying magnetic tape or punched cards for specific, restricted use. If the user discloses the printed document, the software owner may try to prove that the misuse constituted "publication" and, after registering the document, sue for infringement.

William E. Schuyler, Jr., Commissioner of Patents, told a bar meeting at Dallas in 1969 that there was need to protect innovation—the invention of lesser importance—by some means such as that employed by Germany, Japan, and other industrial nations, perhaps under the commerce clause of the Constitution. He said:

> Computer software is a glaring example of the type of innovation where a new form of protection is required. Regardless of whether or not computer programs are proper subject matter for consideration under the patent statute, most computer programs are obvious to a skilled programmer given an objective to be achieved on the basis of certain input and storage data.
>
> Nevertheless, large sums are being expended to create computer software. Unless we find some way to protect the result of that creative effort, dissemination and exchange of the information will be stifled and our progress will be retarded.

Later it was announced that a committee was being formed by the National Council of Patent Law Associations to study the problem of software protection and to draft any legislation that might seem advisable.

In 1968 Edward J. Brenner, Mr. Schuyler's predecessor, had published a request for suggestions on ways to protect computer programs. Among some thirty replies that were received, the most specific proposal came from International Business Machines Corporation, the leading maker of computer "hardware." The following general description of the proposed system was given:

> This report proposes a registration type of system which provides protection for the investment involved in creating a workable program rather than for the discovery of new concepts or new principles. Under the proposed system a registered program cannot be copied, executed, translated, etc., without the owner's authorization.
>
> At the time of registration a copy of the program per se and a description of the concepts used in the program will be deposited with a registrar. At the option of the party who is registering a program, a detailed description of the program (e.g., detailed flow charts, etc.) may also be deposited if one wants to gain protection for this material. The registrar will maintain the program per se and the detailed description in secrecy until the end of the period of protection, but he will make public the description of the concepts. The person who registers a program may attempt to keep the registered program secret or he may divulge the program to any extent that he desires. The only examination required at the time of registration is a determination that the format of the description of the concepts is in proper form.
>
> Unauthorized copy, translation, use or transfer of physical possession of a registered program or of the registered detailed description would subject one to liability. No liability will be incurred under this system by one who uses the published conceptual description to independently create a new program.
>
> This proposal does not involve any changes in the patent system. Thus, the patent system will continue to exist in its present form. If someone believes he has developed a patentable concept, he may seek patent protection for that concept. He could, if he desired, also register the detailed program, providing he disclosed the concept for which patent protection had been requested. However, it is felt that the system being proposed provides a viable alternative for those seeking to protect computer programs, most of which do not involve unobvious concepts.

There would be no examination except as to form and completeness, under the IBM proposal. A fee of about $100 was suggested and the term was to be ten years. A gazette would publish an abstract of each registered program and an indication of the source of licenses.

Some of the thirty-odd other suggestions received by Commissioner Brenner were in general similar to IBM's. Others proposed amendment of the patent law or adaptation of the copyright statute to cover software more fully.

SEXUALLY REPRODUCED PLANTS

Plants that reproduce asexually (by grafting, budding, cuttings, or division) have been protected by patents since 1930. Plant breeders and seed dealers would like protection also for plants that reproduce sexually—that is, by seed.

Bills sponsored by some thirty representatives and a number of senators, introduced late in 1969, would establish in the Department of Agriculture a bureau to be known as the Plant Variety Protection Office, headed by a commissioner. The chief advocate of the project is the American Seed Trade Association. The concept was discussed with the Department of Agriculture, state agricultural experiment directors, the Experiment Station Committee on Organization and Policy, and the Association of Seed Certifying Agencies. The National Association of State Departments of Agriculture, the National Cotton Council, and the National Council of Commercial Plant Breeders endorsed the plan. The new agency would grant a plant variety protection certificate to the breeder or discoverer of any novel variety of sexually reproduced plant (except fungi, bacteria, and hybrids). Known varieties would be excluded.

Roses and carnations are patentable, but cotton and wheat are not. The growers of cotton, rice, wheat, soybeans, and other unpatentable crops believe protection would provide the breeders with revenues for private research into new types. Many cereals, forages, flowers, vegetables, and grasses would be in the same category.

The proposed law would supplement plant patents by adding protection through an agency other than the Patent Office and would leave the patent statute unchanged. In the drafting of the 1930 patent amendment, asexual propagation was specified to prevent a monopoly on the cereal grains. The law also excluded "tuber-propagated plants" (a term later interpreted as meaning Irish potatoes and Jerusalem artichokes) to block monopoly on these foods. The new bill is silent on such plants.

Although the bill proposes an examination system, its backers regard it as offering protection more analagous to that of copyrights than of patents. For immediate protection, a breeder can give notice with the words "Propagation Prohibited" on his labels when he begins distribution. Provisions of the proposed act are as follows:

- The term is seventeen years (the same as for plant patents).
- The applicant agrees that a viable sample of basic seed necessary for propagation of the variety will be deposited and replenished periodically in a public repository.
- Holders of certificates are to affix to containers labels including the words "U.S. Protected Variety."
- The right is given to exclude others from selling the variety, offering it for sale, or reproducing, importing, or exporting it; remedy for infringement is by civil action.
- The Secretary of Agriculture may compel licensing on a reasonable basis in order to insure an adequate supply of fiber, food, or feed in this country.
- Rights are not infringed by a farmer who saves seed and grows the variety for his own use.
- A Plant Variety Protection Board, including industry representatives, makes advisory decisions on appeals from the examiners and advises the commissioner of the Plant Variety

Protection Office and the Secretary of Agriculture on various other matters.

- Protection is limited to United States nationals except for countries that grant reciprocity.
- An official journal is authorized.
- Fees include $50 upon filing and $50 upon issuance.
- A certificate may be opened to reexamination within five years after issuance.
- The act takes effect when approved.

At this writing, the prospects for broadened plant protection are uncertain.* Even on a new design law and revision of the copyright statute, which have been pending for years, prophecy is dangerous, as the legislative process is slow. But in general the innovator still has some choice of procedures. He may want to rely on copyrights or trade secrets or (to avoid patenting) fast marketing.

NOTE: In December, 1970, after this chapter had been set in type, Congress passed and the President signed an act substantially as outlined but specifically excepting from coverage okra, celery, peppers, tomatoes, carrots, and cucumbers. The Secretary of Agriculture was to fix the fees, but until he did so the filing fee was to be $50.

VII

The Patent Office and Other Federal Agencies

From the White House down, the executive branch of the government has always been interested in the patent system. George Washington signed the first U.S. patent law and the first patent issued. Abraham Lincoln, himself the inventor of a device for buoying vessels over shoals, wrote the much-quoted words with which this book begins: "The patent system added the fuel of interest to the fire of genius."

In recent years, Presidential decisions regarding the patent system have been important. Harry S. Truman's 1950 executive order covers rights to federal employees' inventions. John F. Kennedy's 1963 statement of government patent policy is generally followed in the allocation of rights to patents arising from federal research and development contracts. A President's Commission on the Patent System, appointed by Lyndon B. Johnson in 1965, recommended "reform" legislation, which is still pending in modified draft. And in 1970, at the request of Richard M. Nixon, the Senate gave its consent to a convention creating the World Intellectual Property Organization (patents are considered intellectual property).

The federal departments and agencies have direct interests in the system through exclusive or partial rights that they hold to patents obtained by their employees or contractors. The defense agencies watch for inventions they can use and demand secrecy on those whose publication as patents might adversely affect the national security. The legislative and judicial branches of government are often concerned with patents when new laws are proposed or when disputes get into court.

The Patent Office has both direct and indirect relationships with other agencies and departments. Staff patent attorneys in many federal offices represent employees and their agencies in the "prosecution" of patent applications and in related matters. The Patent Office, as required by law, has direct contacts with the defense agencies in regard to secrecy. Two government departments regularly help patent examiners in their work. The Department of Health, Education, and Welfare (HEW) gives direct assistance on applications for drug patents. The Federal Food, Drug, and Cosmetic Act instructs HEW to conduct necessary research and furnish complete information in response to requests. Under a Presidential directive, the Department of Agriculture aids in evaluating plant patents. When applications are submitted to it, Agriculture gives its opinion as to whether a variety is new. The Patent Office, however, is not bound by the Department's opinion.

Many indirect relationships with other departments come about because of the Patent Office's product (patents) and its clients (inventors). The Department of Justice, for example, may bring antitrust suits that affect patents and their owners but do not involve the Patent Office as such.

White House Link

The President's Commission on the Patent System went out of existence after its report was presented to President Lyndon B. Johnson in 1966, but another group, which receives little public notice, has kept a White House eye on the patent system since 1963—the Federal Council for Science and Technology, part of the Executive Office of the President. The Kennedy policy statement of 1963 ordered that the council prepare a report at least annually, in consultation with the Department of Justice. The report was to cover the effectiveness of the policy and include any recommendations for necessary revision. President Kennedy also directed the council to establish a patent advisory panel to make detailed studies. Accordingly, the council set up an advisory panel of working-level agency representatives and in 1965 established a committee on government patent policy whose members included high-level officials from the research and development agencies represented on the council. (In 1969 the panel and the committee were merged.)

Reports for 1965–1968 have been published, as well as a government patent policy study prepared for the committee by Harbridge House, Inc., of Boston and published in 1968. This $350,000 study, which was ordered by the Department of Commerce on behalf of the patent policy committee, examined the effects of patent policy on industry participation in government research and development programs, on commercial utilization of government-sponsored inventions, and on business competition in commercial markets but did not cover operations of the Patent Office itself.

Observers had expected that the Harbridge House study and the research of the committee on government patent policy would bring recommendations for federal legislation setting over-all policy on research and development patents, but at this writing no bill had been offered by either the Johnson or Nixon Administration. In 1966 the Senate Judiciary Committee reported out its own bill to fix patent policy, but it was not adopted.

Although it does not bear directly on Patent Office procedure, the Kennedy policy on federal contracts does affect the nature of the American patent system by regulating the ownership of many thousands of inventions. The Kennedy statement, issued October 10, 1963, provides in general that when inventions are intended for commercial use by the public, when they concern the public health or welfare, when they might give a contractor a dominant position, or when they result from operation of a federal facility, the government shall acquire principal rights and grant licenses to potential users. When a contractor already has an established commercial position in the area, he is to get principal rights, granting the government a license for its purposes. If, however, the contractor does not "work" the invention within three years, he may be required to grant royalty-free, nonexclusive licenses to others.

To the extent that they are not bound by specific legislation, government agencies have tried to apply the Kennedy policy to their own fields. The degree to which an agency insists on full title depends in part on its purpose in encouraging inventions. The Department of Defense, for example, wants weapons created for its own use, not for public use.

FEDERAL EMPLOYEE INVENTORS

The policy on rights to inventions made by government employees was set by President Harry S. Truman in Executive Order 10096, issued January 23, 1950. Under this, the government acquires title to all inventions made by any government employee "(1) during working hours, or (2) with a contribution by the government of facilities, equipment, materials, funds, or information, or of time or services of other government employees on official duty, or (3) which bear a direct relation to or are made in consequence of the official duties of the inventor." When the government contribution is such that it would be inequitable for it to take title, or when it has no interest in the invention, the government may retain only a royalty-free, nonexclusive, irrevocable license for its purposes. If the government does not assert any rights or request a license, the entire title is left with the employee.

An earlier Truman order directed that agencies, "whenever practicable," acquire the right to file foreign patent applications on inventions resulting from federally conducted or financed research. In practice, the claim for full title is enforced only against employees engaged in research and development. Often, if the government takes only a license, the inventor is given domestic and foreign commercial rights.

Under regulations approved by President Kennedy in 1962, the Commissioner of Patents reviews cases involving an employee's domestic (but not foreign) rights and may revise the terms. In disputes, employees can appeal to the Commissioner and if necessary take the matter to court. The order applies to all agencies except the Atomic Energy Commission. (The Atomic Energy Commission's Patent Compensation Board and the National Aeronautics and Space Administration's Inventions and Contributions Board are discussed separately below.)

Both civilian employees of the government and military personnel are entitled to awards for special contributions or services, including inventions. Department of Defense agencies give civilian and armed service inventors $50 at filing and $100 at issuance of a patent, and a number of nondefense agencies make similar payments. In addition to these nominal sums, an agency may make a cash award up to $5,000 to a civilian; with the approval of the Civil Service Commission this may be increased to $25,000 for an individual or group without special congressional action. In the case of military personnel, awards between $5,000 and $25,000 must be approved by the Assistant Secretary of Defense for Manpower and Reserve Affairs.

As to secrecy, the U.S. patent law provides that when issuance of a patent on an invention in which the government has a property interest might, in the opinion of the interested federal agency, be detrimental to national security, the Patent Commissioner shall, upon request of a defense agency, keep it secret and delay granting the patent. If the government has no property interest but the Commissioner thinks publication might be detrimental, he is to show the application to representatives of the Atomic Energy Commission, Department of Defense, or any other designated defense agency. (Under the 1958 National Aeronautics and Space Act, NASA is such an agency.) Upon request, a secrecy order is issued.

Secrecy orders generally remain in force for a year and are renewable for the same period. In time of war or national emergency, a secrecy order is in force until a year after termination of hostilities. An order may be rescinded if the interested agency approves. An applicant has a right of appeal from a secrecy order to the Secretary of Commerce. He is entitled to compensation from the government for use of an invention that is kept secret—if the patent is allowed—from the date of first use.

Officers and employees of the Patent Office are prohibited by law, during their appointments or for one year thereafter, from applying for a patent or acquiring any patent rights, except by inheritance or bequest.

ATOMIC ENERGY INVENTIONS

The Atomic Energy Act of 1954 prohibits the granting of patents for "any invention or discovery which is useful solely in the utilization of special nuclear material or atomic energy in an atomic weapon." If a patent application for such a weapon invention is filed, the Patent Office is required to furnish a copy to the Atomic Energy Commission (AEC). Applicants for atomic energy patents are required to file affidavits on the making or conception of the inventions, and copies are sent to the AEC for determination as to whether the inventions were made under contract. The AEC may also declare a patent in the atomic energy field "affected with the public interest" and, subject to hearings, may acquire a license for its own use with the right to license others in limited circumstances. The AEC seldom finds it necessary to request imposition of secrecy orders on nonweapon applications. It owns inventions made by its contractors, unless it waives the rights. A Patent Compensation Board rules on royalties and compensation for patent holders and inventors of weapons and other atomic energy inventions. The AEC can also make awards to persons not entitled to royalties or compensation. With the approval of the President, awards may be made "for any especially meritorious contribution to the development, use, or control of atomic energy."

Since its establishment in 1946, the Atomic Energy Commission has conducted its research, development, and production largely through contracts with industrial firms and universities for the operation of government-owned facilities and has acquired principal rights to several thousand patents. Royalty-free nonexclusive licenses are granted on AEC-owned domestic patents. These patents cover all phases of the atomic energy field, including nuclear reactors and components, fuel element fabrication and reprocessing, processes for producing source materials, special nuclear materials, and a great many radiation detection and measurement devices, other instruments, and a wide variety of mechanical equipment and apparatus.

Many of the inventions are in technical areas of interest to industry outside the atomic energy field. These include welding and brazing apparatus, special metal alloys, electronic circuits, nondestructive testing equipment, precision machining, and gauging. Some of the patents relate to uses of radioisotopes in such fields as medicine, industrial gauging, and irradiation of materials. Licenses may also be obtained to patents owned by AEC in a score of foreign countries.

UNDER THE SPACE LAW

The National Aeronautics and Space Act of 1958 provides that inventions made under contracts with the National Aeronautics and Space Administration (NASA) will be exclusive government property unless NASA waives all or part of the rights. All NASA contracts require the disclosure to that agency of any invention, discovery, improvement, or innovation made in performance of the work.

If an application for a patent not assigned to the NASA Administrator appears to the Commissioner of Patents to have significance in aeronautical or space activities, the inventor is required to file an affidavit describing the circumstances under which the invention was made and any relationship to a NASA contract. NASA reviews the application and affidavit and can request issuance of the patent to the agency, subject to a hearing. Even after a patent is awarded, the NASA Administrator can reopen the case and request reassignment of the patent to NASA, subject to proof of misrepresentation in the affidavit.

Because of the wording of the Space Act, a good many patents for inventions made under NASA contracts are issued in the name of the agency's current Administrator "with respect to an invention of" the contractor's employee who made it. This wording is far from popular. A study made for NASA in 1966 by George Washington University reported that inventors disliked seeing the Administrator's name on patents for their inventions.

A NASA Inventions and Contributions Board reviews requests for waiver of rights by NASA and makes recommendations to the Administrator. The board also makes cash awards for significant scientific or technical contributions. No award may be made for more than $100,000 unless NASA has reported the circumstances to the appropriate committees of Congress and waited thirty calendar days during a regular session. The largest single award ever given by the NASA Board was $35,000.

NASA may grant licenses under patents and patent applications that it owns (assigned to the agency by contractors or its employees), or it may grant waivers of commercial rights to the contractors, retaining a license for itself. The NASA licenses are usually nonexclusive and are granted without fee; however, a few exclusive licenses have been granted when no use resulted from nonexclusive arrangements. An exclusive licensee pays nothing but agrees to spend a specified sum of money on commercial development of the licensed invention.

In March, 1969, NASA announced that it had issued the first royalty-bearing license under its foreign patent program. The agreement granted to the Nippon Electric Company, Ltd., of Tokyo an exclusive license for manufacture in Japan of a metal connection for solar cells, protected by a NASA-owned Japanese patent. The down payment was $2,000, and Nippon Electric undertook to pay royalties of 1 per cent of sales for the duration of the agreement. By the end of 1969 NASA had chosen 36 inventions as important enough to protect abroad and had filed a total of 282 patent applications on them in one or more of 11 countries. At that time the agency had received 122 foreign patents, and others were still pending.

NASA's Office of Technology Utilization spreads word of by-product space inventions that industry and medicine may use. Besides those disclosed in patents, many are summarized in *Tech Briefs* (brief reports of recent innovations) or presented in more detail in other NASA publications. By January, 1970, NASA had printed more than 3,000 *Tech Briefs* announcing innovations of potential commercial use in every field of technology, and had published a list of 1,040 patents available for licensing. These so-called spin-off developments included sharper X-ray pictures, longer-lasting paints, safer highways, improved ambulance service, tougher metals, smaller TV cameras, new metalworking tools, and miniature medical instruments.

DEPARTMENT OF DEFENSE PATENT PRACTICES

The three big spenders of research and development funds are the Department of Defense, NASA, and the Atomic Energy Commission. Defense, unlike the other two agencies, has no special law governing its invention and patenting activities.

Some agencies sponsor research to develop articles and processes for public use, and in general retain title to patents so that they can grant nonexclusive licenses to anyone interested. The Department of Defense, on the other hand, develops principally weapons systems; its rifles and tanks are not intended for the office or household. End items of its development programs, such as industrial diamonds, in which there might be some commercial interest, are few and far between. In most cases, therefore, the Army, Navy, and Air Force retain only rights for government use of the invention and leave the principal title with the contractor, who may be able to find some incidental commercial applications.

In the year 1966, for which figures are available, the Department of Defense had 21,449 prime contracts containing patent rights clauses (some 13,000 were Air Force contracts). In 82 per cent of these cases, Defense kept only a license, leaving principal rights with the contractor. In 7 per cent, Defense retained title, and, in 11 per cent, the Department had a deferred right to claim title. Four out of five contracts, therefore, made the contractor the principal patent owner.

INVENTIONS FOR PUBLIC USE

The Department of Health, Education, and Welfare, the Department of Agriculture, the Department of the Interior, and the Federal Aviation Administration normally acquire title to patents resulting from their programs, with a view to licensing private commercial users.

HEW makes exceptions, however, for nonprofit educational institutions that administer patents in a manner regarded by the Department as in the public interest and for industrial organizations active in the cancer chemotherapy program. In fiscal 1966, the holders of 5,910 grants and contracts, out of a total of 30,269, were given first option to acquire title. In its statement of general policy, HEW notes that inventions developed through its resources and activities are a potential resource of great value to the public health and welfare. The policy is

(a) To safeguard the public interest in inventions developed by Department employees, contractors and grantees with the aid of public funds and facilities;

(b) To encourage and recognize individual and cooperative achievement in research and investigations; and

(c) To establish a procedure, consistent with pertinent statutes, Executive Orders and general Government regulations, for the determination of rights and obligations relating to the patenting of inventions.

The Assistant Secretary for Health and Scientific Affairs has broad authority to determine the disposition of rights to inventions reported under grants and contracts. Subject only to specific requirements of statutes and executive orders, he may

1) Permit the grantee or contractor to retain title where he finds that "the invention will either be effectively dedicated to the public . . . or generally available for royalty-free and non-exclusive licensing . . .";

2) Assign title to a "competent organization" for development and administration where he finds that (a) this will more adequately and quickly develop the invention for widest use and (b) adequate safeguards exist against unreasonable royalties and repressive practices;

3) Leave disposition of patent rights to another government agency that has contributed to the work;
4) Require title to be assigned to the government.

Some indication of the importance attached to the office of Assistant Secretary for Health and Scientific Affairs was given in the summer of 1969 when a political controversy developed over filling the post, and Dr. Roger O. Egeberg was nominated by President Nixon after Secretary Robert H. Finch's first choice, Dr. John H. Knowles, had been opposed by conservatives in the Senate and by organized medicine.

The Department of Agriculture, whose policy is to retain for the United States the domestic title to inventions resulting from employee research and worldwide title from contractor research, has had a long relationship with the Patent Office. Henry L. Ellsworth, the first to hold the title Commissioner of Patents, was also the first federal official to attempt to promote agriculture. In 1836 he began to distribute plants and seeds of value to farmers. Before creation of the Department of Agriculture, the Patent Office had an agricultural division; it also gathered meteorological data. In 1862, when Congress created an agricultural agency with bureau status, its first head and other personnel were drawn from the Patent Office.

Most of the department's extensive research is of a public service nature, and the patented inventions that result are predominantly for use by private agriculture and industry, rather than by the government itself. As a consequence, it is established departmental policy that an invention resulting from the agency's research must be made freely available to the public on a royalty-free, nonexclusive basis. The Plant Patent Act of 1930 provided that the Commissioner of Patents might request the assistance of the Department of Agriculture in regard to such patents. President Herbert Hoover directed that the Department make information available and authorized the performance of necessary research and the detailing of officers and employees for this purpose. Employment contracts provide that employees shall not help anyone prepare or prosecute plant patent applications or advise whether a plant is new. Inquiries are referred to the Patent Office. The Department of the Interior's research programs are intended primarily for the benefit of the public rather than for government procurement. In accordance with the Kennedy statement and specific provisions in such laws as the Saline Water Act and the Coal Research Act, Interior normally acquires principal rights. Title is sometimes left with a contractor if he has a well-established background in the technology and a commercial position. Of 522 prime contracts awarded in 1966, only thirteen gave the contractors first option to acquire title, and in three cases the allocation of rights was deferred. Department policy is to grant licenses that do not require royalty payments. An exception is made when a licensee brings suit against the government for patent infringement on patents that he holds. In this case, Interior feels it is entitled to a reasonable royalty charge under its license by way of a counterclaim.

The Tennessee Valley Authority (TVA) is a public corporation whose patent activities were specified in the 1933 law creating it. Among its objects are the development of improved fertilizer products and processes. The law authorized TVA to request the assistance and advice of employees or officers of any federal agency "to enable the Corporation the better to carry out its powers successfully." There is an added provision that "any invention or discovery made by virtue of and incidental to such service by an employee of the Government of the United States [so serving], or by any employee of the Corporation, together with any patents which may be granted thereon, shall be the sole and exclusive property of the Corporation." A further clause authorized payments to inventors from the sale of licenses, but in practice the licenses have been royalty-free.

TVA decided it was required to assert title only to those employee inventions made by virtue of and incidental to their services and makes exceptions when it is not interested in the invention, retaining only a license. It is authorized to make contracts for research and development, but very few patentable inventions have resulted from such work. Almost all of TVA's patents have been based on inventions made by its employees.

Although in recent years it has not had occasion to request such information, the 1933 law empowered TVA to obtain information from Patent Office records (not including pending applications) on the production of fixed nitrogen—or any essential ingredient of fertilizer—and hydroelectric power production. Patent owners whose patent rights were used or infringed were to recover compensation through United States district courts.

The 1950 law creating the National Science Foundation directs that no officer or employee "shall acquire, retain, or transfer any rights, under the patent laws of the United States or otherwise, in any invention which he may make or produce in connection with performing his assigned activities and which is directly related to the subject matter thereof." An added proviso says this shall not prevent an officer or employee from executing patent applications assigned to the government. Although the foundation makes about 9,000 grants a year, most of them relate to basic research, and relatively few patentable inventions are produced. Rather than determining in advance where title is to rest, the foundation's contracts regularly defer the determination of patent rights until an invention has been identified.

Helping Hands: The National Bureau of Standards

The National Bureau of Standards (NBS), a sister agency in the Department of Commerce, works with both the Patent Office and its clients, the inventors.

An Office of Invention and Innovation in the NBS encourages state inventors' exhibitions, gives staff support to a body of private citizens called the National Inventors Council, and seeks out federal policies likely to promote technological advances. Popular interest has been aroused in new products and processes through the state invention expositions promoted by the Office of Invention and Innovation. Between ten and fifteen are held every year, and twenty-four states have put on at least one show. This NBS unit arranges with the Patent Office and other agencies to supply speakers. Exhibitors are advised to display working models but are advised to get patent protection first. An exposition involves a 2- or 3-day meeting designed to bring together inventors, patent owners, manufacturers, distributors, investors, and the buying public, so that patents can be sold or licensed and arrangements can be made for the production and distribution of new inventions and products. The states are the usual sponsors, often with participation by universities, bar and technical associations, and chambers of commerce. The Office of Invention and Innovation (address: National Bureau of Standards, Washington, D.C., 20234) will upon request supply guidelines and examples of typical registration forms, programs, award certificates, and terminal questionnaires.

If anyone wants to sell a patent or concept to the government but does not know where to address the proposal, the Office of Invention and Innovation will forward his offer. Its folder, *How to Submit Ideas and Inventions to the United States Government,* says that a trip to Washington is not the best way to proceed, because the expert who passes on a proposal may be in a distant laboratory. Daniel V. De Simone is the head of the Office of Invention and Innovation.*

* Mr. De Simone is also executive director of the National Inventors Council, whose chairman is Dr. Charles Stark Draper, president of the Charles Stark Draper Laboratory Division, Massachusetts Institute of Technology. The council was organized in 1940 with Charles F. Kettering (in-

Technical aid is provided to the Patent Office by the NBS Center for Computer Sciences and Technology at Gaithersburg, Maryland. Joint studies with the Patent Office have been conducted on methods of mechanizing the searching of patents—that is, on harnessing the computer to take over the examiner's manual job of sorting patents and technical literature to find out whether what is claimed in a patent application is really new. Progress has been made in mechanized searching in the important and complex field of chemicals. Under the name of Operation Haystaq, computer programs were devised for fast and efficient storage, conversion, and retrieval of chemical information. One problem was to describe not only the constituents of chemical compounds but their three-dimensional structures. Specialists succeeded in representing such a structure by a string of characters with only one dimension, which were therefore capable of digital encoding for input to computers.

For the Inventor-Businessman

The Patent Office has friends in the many field offices of the Department of Commerce and Small Business Administration (SBA). Advice on developing and marketing inventions is dispensed by both types of offices. The Commerce offices have Patent Office publications; the SBA offers its own booklets and also—something of great importance to the inventor starting production in a garage—loans. A publication bearing directly on invention, *Know Your Patenting Procedure*, can be obtained free from any SBA office. Under its technology utilization program, the SBA also distributes NASA's *Tech*

---

ventor of the self-starter) as chairman and Orville Wright (co-inventor of the airplane) as one of the members. The council, which consists of leading inventors, industrial executives, and patent lawyers, advises the Secretary of Commerce on federal policies that will stimulate invention, benefit society by putting inventions to work, and protect the interests of inventors.

Briefs, mentioned above, and similar publications issued by the Atomic Energy Commission covering inventions and technical advances in special fields, as well as summaries of research and development patents owned by the government.

Decisions on SBA loans for innovation (the introduction of a new product or process) are made in the field, without the necessity of referral to Washington. The law authorizes the Small Business Administration to help small firms undertake joint programs for research and development. Among the purposes of such ventures are the prosecution of patent applications, the furnishing of patent services to participants, the granting of licenses, and the formation of corporations to exploit particular patents. Such joint projects, however, are seldom undertaken.

THE DEPARTMENT OF JUSTICE AND THE COURTS

The solicitor of the Patent Office, through the general counsel of the Commerce Department, cooperates with the Department of Justice and calls its attention to apparent violations of federal laws. If a petition to the Supreme Court for a writ of certiorari seems to be in order in connection with a court decision involving the Commissioner of Patents, this is taken up with the solicitor general in the Justice Department.

Patents, since they represent a limited monopoly, are sometimes misused and therefore become involved in antitrust actions brought by the Justice Department, but the Patent Office itself is not involved in such suits.* In January, 1970, a new patent unit was formed in Justice's Antitrust Division to handle restrictive practices in the licensing of patents and technology. It was announced that the Justice Department had

---

* The dividing line between limited monopoly and restraint of competition as defined by the antitrust laws is sometimes difficult to distinguish. The subject is discussed in more detail in Chapter X ("Controversies").

in recent months challenged the legality of a number of patent and know-how licensing practices, including (1) restrictions against the sale of generic or bulk drugs, (2) agreements not to contest the validity of patents, and (3) agreements dividing fields-of-use.

The Patent Office solicitor represents the Commissioner in the District Court for the District of Columbia, where all civil actions to compel issuance of a patent must be brought. Certain other civil actions against the Commissioner, involving procedural matters, may be brought in any jurisdiction where the plaintiff lives. In such a case, the Commissioner is represented by the United States attorney in the particular district. As mentioned in Chapter III, patent applicants dissatisfied with decisions made in the Patent Office may appeal to, or start civil actions in, certain courts, and patent owners often sue for infringement.

OTHER FEDERAL AGENCIES

The Patent Office deals directly with several departments and agencies not so far mentioned. Its income—chiefly receipts from fees and from the sales of patent and trademark copies—is paid into the Treasury, which meets the payroll and expenses from appropriations. The General Accounting Office, a congressional watchdog, examines Patent Office salaries and expenses. The General Services Administration (GSA), the government housekeeping agency, is the Patent Office landlord. GSA's National Archives and Records Service is the repository for noncurrent and historical Patent Office records, some dating back to the eighteenth century. On international patent and trademark affairs, there is a close partnership with the Department of State, as indicated in Chapter V. And, like other federal agencies, the Patent Office works with the Civil Service Commission in personnel matters (see Appendix A on Career Opportunities).

The Government Printing Office produces copies of patents and all the reports, booklets, and other publications of the Patent Office and distributes everything except the patent and trademark copies. Recently, as mentioned in Chapters III and XI, the Government Printing Office has begun printing patents and other documents by a computerized process.

Patentees and trademark registrants may have occasion to deal with other federal offices. If a trademark or trade name of American ownership (even if of foreign origin) is recorded with the Treasury Department, the Treasury's Bureau of Customs prohibits the importation of merchandise bearing a mark or name that copies or simulates it. The owner of a U.S. patent who believes merchandise is being imported that infringes the patent can apply to the Bureau of Customs for a survey. He must furnish a certified copy of the patent, as well as 600 printed copies for distribution to ports of entry, and pay a fee. The bureau will conduct a survey for two, four, or six months, as the applicant elects, and furnish him with the names and addresses of importers of merchandise that appears to infringe the patent. The patent owner may decide to settle the matter through an infringement suit, or he may request an investigation by the U.S. Tariff Commission. If the commission finds that there has been infringement, it can recommend to the President that the merchandise be excluded. If the President so rules, the Bureau of Customs will carry out the order.

Whatever connection exists between the Patent Office and the Smithsonian Institution is chiefly historical and sentimental. The Smithsonian now occupies, among its many structures, what Washington generally knows as the Old Patent Office Building. The vast Smithsonian collections include hundreds of old patent models, which until 1880 were generally required with patent applications. And the Smithsonian is a rich source of information on the development of the technical as well as the decorative arts.

VIII

Patents and Congress

With paternal watchfulness, Congress holds the Patent Office's purse strings and regulates the agency's conduct. Like all federal agencies, the Patent Office looks to Capitol Hill for appropriations. Under the broad authority of the Constitution, Congress passes the laws that control its organization and operation. Currently there are two sets of committees to be dealt with regularly—the Appropriations Committees of both houses, which handle the detailed Patent Office arithmetic, and the Senate and House Judiciary Committees, which handle groundwork on statutory changes. Actually, Patent Office contacts are with subcommittees: in the Senate with the Judiciary Committee's Subcommittee on Patents, Trademarks, and Copyrights and in the House with the Judiciary Committee's Subcommittee No. 3, which has special jurisdiction over patents, trademarks, copyrights, and revision of the laws.

Hearings before the Judiciary committees are generally formal and polite, but on the House side the questioning of officials about money matters has sometimes been severe. Since 1961 Senator John L. McClellan of Arkansas has headed both the Senate's Judiciary subcommittee and the Senate Appropriations subcommittee that considers Patent Office funds. The main work on financing the agency, however, is done in the House of Representatives, where appropriations originate.

The Senate Subcommittee on Patents, Trademarks, and Copyrights has conducted many detailed studies and held hearings not only on proposed legislation but on how the American patent system works and how it ought to work. Thirty research reports written by outside specialists or staff members of the Library of Congress Legislative Reference Service have been published to date. The titles of these reports are listed in the Bibliography. Although many bills have been introduced by Senator McClellan and other members of both houses since the codification of the patent law effected in 1952, few have been enacted. The American patent system, which has suited so many people for so long, is slow to change.

The House Judiciary Subcommittee No. 3 was set up in 1946. Its work relating to patents had its roots in a standing committee with a long history. In the first session of the Twenty-fifth Congress, on September 15, 1837, Congress "raised" a Committee on Patents, with jurisdiction at that time confined to patents alone. Jurisdiction over copyrights and trademarks was added on motion of John S. Newberry of Michigan in the second session of the Forty-sixth Congress, called to order December 1, 1879. Jurisdiction was transferred to the Judiciary Committee in the reorganization act of 1946. The subcommittee is headed at this writing by Representative Robert W. Kastenmeier of Wisconsin; Representative Richard H. Poff of Virginia is an active member. Unlike the Senate subcommittee, the House subcommittee has not published any general studies of the patent system.

PATENT LEGISLATION

The present patent law (Appendix B) is substantially the law as codified in 1952, when the statutes were completely rewritten for the first time since 1870. The new text, which was the work of both House and Senate Judiciary committees, took into account various court decisions and was rearranged to provide a simpler and a better working tool.

Section 103, consisting of only two sentences, aroused discussion on several points. Had it lowered the standard of patentability previously laid down by the Supreme Court? And what about "nonobviousness" and the "flash of genius"? The section follows:

> A patent may not be obtained though the invention is not identically disclosed or described as set forth in section 102 of this title, if the differences between the subject matter sought to be patented and the prior art are such that the subject matter as a whole would have been obvious at the time the invention was made to a person having ordinary skill in the art to which said subject matter pertains. Patentability shall not be negatived by the manner in which the invention was made.

In a 1966 decision (*Graham* v. *John Deere Company*), the Supreme Court found that the standard of patentability had not been lowered. "We have concluded," said the court, "that the 1952 Act was intended to codify judicial precedents embracing the principle long ago announced by this Court in *Hotchkiss* v. *Greenwood* . . . (1850), and that, while the clear language of [Section] 103 places emphasis on an inquiry into obviousness, the general level of innovation necessary to sustain patentability remains the same."

The court said elsewhere, "We have been urged to find in [Section] 103 a relaxed standard supposedly a congressional reaction to the 'increased standard' applied by this Court in its decisions over the last 20 or 30 years. The standard has remained invariable in this Court."

In its 1966 opinion, the court voiced no disagreement with the provision that patentability shall not be negatived by the manner of invention. This disposed of a widely held impression, arising from a controversial 1941 decision of the same court, that invention must result from a "flash of creative genius," and not mere laboratory research or happy accident. An act passed in 1965 changed Patent Office fees for the first time since 1932, raising them to a scale that was expected to reimburse the Treasury for about three-quarters of the agency's expenses. Today's rates are a far cry from those imposed when the American patent system was founded. Under the 1790 law, fees were as follows:

Receiving and filing petitions	$ .50
Filing specifications, per copy sheet containing 100 words	.10
Making out a patent	2.00
Affixing Great Seal	1.00
Endorsing the day of delivering the patent to the patentee, including all intermediate services	.20

From this nominal scale, fees were gradually increased. The 1965 amendment raised the patent filing fee from $30 to $65, plus charges depending on the number of claims and the manner of their presentation, and raised the issuance fee from $30 to $100, plus charges depending on the number of pages of specification and drawings. The new law required other agencies for the first time to pay fees for patents applied for by them, and at the same scale as the public, except that the Commissioner of Patents might waive payment for occasional services. Other provisions, which were aimed at expediting examination, recognized a claim dependent on a preceding claim and required payment of the issue fee, or part of it, within three months after the notice of allowance.

The Patent Office estimated that at the new scale an inventor would pay $229 in fees for a patent of average size, plus his attorney's charges.

The Senate created its Judiciary Subcommittee on Patents, Trademarks, and Copyrights in 1955 and authorized it to conduct a full and complete examination of the Patent Office and the patent statutes. The first chairman was Senator Joseph C. O'Mahoney of Wyoming; he was succeeded in 1961 by the present chairman, Senator McClellan. A 1958 law approved by the subcommittee gave the Commissioner of Patents a raise in pay from $16,000 to $20,000 (it is now $36,000). Lifting the ceiling on the Commissioner's salary permitted promotions for other officers. The Act also increased the number of members of the Patent Office Board of Appeals from nine to fifteen and approved the same compensation for acting members as for regular members. The subcommittee also supported a 1958 Act providing for new flexibility in assignments for judges of the Court of Customs and Patent Appeals and judges of the Court of Claims.

In 1961 a law was enacted to carry into effect revised provisions of the Convention of Paris for the Protection of Industrial Property and to authorize observance of the 125th anniversary of the Patent Act of 1836. In 1964 a private law was enacted authorizing payment of $100,000 to Frank B. Rowlett for cryptologic inventions that he had been unable to patent because of their secret nature. Other laws adopted at about the same time extended the terms of design patents protecting a plaque and medal of the American Legion, the insignia of the United Daughters of the Confederacy, and the insignia of the Massachusetts Department of the United American Veterans of the United States of America, Inc. As of 1970, the most important pending legislation is the so-called patent reform bill. It is examined in Chapter X ("Controversies").

The Judiciary subcommittees have considered a large number of bills never adopted. The subjects include a uniform policy as to ownership of patents resulting from federal research and development contracts or covering inventions of federal employees, as well as proposals to make the Patent Office an independent agency (see Chapter X). The Senate Judiciary Committee favorably reported a bill by Senator

Alexander Wiley of Wisconsin to make Irish potatoes eligible for plant patents, but no action was taken by the Senate.

The proposal to fix by law a single patent policy for all government agencies has received much study in both houses. Senator McClellan and others introduced bills designed to establish it. Fifteen staff reports were made for his committee on the practices of individual agencies. But throughout the government such operations continue to be guided by orders of Presidents Truman and Kennedy, as described in the preceding chapter, except as fixed in specific legislation for certain agencies or projects.

The Senate Committee on Foreign Relations has an important role in the consideration of international treaties and conventions relating to patents and trademarks. In 1969 the committee reported favorably a resolution, later passed by both houses, to authorize funds for the 1970 Washington diplomatic conference on a Patent Cooperation Treaty. Upon recommendation of the committee, the Senate in 1970 gave its advice and consent to ratification of the convention establishing the World Intellectual Property Organization (WIPO) and of the revised Paris Convention for the Protection of Intellectual Property (see Chapter V). In the same year, a necessary amendment of the U.S. patent law, recognizing inventors' certificates, came before the Senate Judiciary subcommittee.

A number of other congressional bodies have held hearings and considered bills affecting patents, especially on rights to inventions resulting from federally funded research. These include the Senate Select Committee on Small Business and the House Committee on Science and Astronautics.

CONGRESSIONAL CRITICISM OF THE PATENT SYSTEM

Some Patent Office problems seem to be perennial, and one of these is the time lag between the filing of an application and issuance of a patent. A legislative history, *Expediting Patent Office Procedure*, prepared by the Library of Congress and published by the Senate Subcommittee on Patents, Trademarks, and Copyrights in 1960, tells of long congressional concern at the delay. As early as 1848 the House of Representatives ordered its Committee on Patents to inquire into the causes of delay in examining applications. The committee report commented that the number of applications per examiner was increasing year by year and recommended additional examiners. Two years later a Congressman remarked that "for many years inventors and others have experienced much vexation and inconvenience by reason of the imperfect operations of the law of 1836." He reported that so oppressive had the operation of the patent laws become that in 1845 a national convention had assembled in New York "to take measures to remedy these evils."

The 1836 law was amended as to procedure four times in the 1860's, prior to a general recodification in 1870. The Library of Congress study lists six general acts and nineteen bills (introduced but not enacted) —from 1790 on— bearing directly on the problem and many others with less direct impact. Senator O'Mahoney, in his introduction to the study, said that the lag between filing and issuance averaged in 1960 between three and four years "and in extreme cases has been known to run for decades."

A questionnaire prepared by the Senate Subcommittee on Patents, Trademarks, and Copyrights was sent to a group of independent inventors—persons who had received unassigned patents during parts of 1960 and 1964. They were asked whether they regarded patent procedures as (a) satisfactory as they existed; (b) too complicated, slow, and expensive, but requiring only minor revisions; (c) unsatisfactory and requiring major revisions.

About 60 per cent of the inventors answering indicated that the procedures were too complicated, slow, and expensive but that only minor revisions were required. Approximately 24 per cent found existing procedures satisfactory, while 16 per cent were of the view that the procedures were very unsatisfactory and needed major revisions. Some 36 per cent indicated that their experience had discouraged them from seeking additional patents.

On the proposal for deferred examination, such as that provided in the Netherlands and West Germany, the independents who had any opinion were almost equally divided. A majority opposed a suggestion that a new class of patents be created covering inventions that constituted only minor improvements and on which patents would be issued for a term shorter than the regular seventeen years, but a substantial majority endorsed a proposed amendment to fix the term of a patent at twenty years from the filing date. In a 1965 report, the Senate subcommittee noted:

In comments submitted to the subcommittee the inventors expressed particular concern with the expense and delays involved in securing a patent. The high cost of legal fees was frequently cited. While some of the industry replies urged the Patent Office to be guided by a higher standard of patentability, a common complaint of the inventors was that the Patent Office was too concerned with citing irrelevant prior art and too occupied with technical rules of practice. Reference was also made to the difficulties which an inventor encounters in attempting to sell an invention before the patent has issued. A number of inventors referred to difficulties with corporations either in trying to interest them in an invention or because of alleged infringement by corporations. There was considerable sentiment in favor of greater assistance by the Government to the inventor, particularly in aiding him with funds to commercially market his invention. While the subcommittee questionnaire was not directed toward employee-inventors, certain respondents expressed considerable dissatisfaction with the terms of employment agreements restricting the patent rights of employee-inventors.

The general attitude of the patent bar and Patent Office staff toward the patent system has been one of reverence. Over several years, the Senate subcommittee sought the opinions of economists as to the system's contributions to economic growth and inventive activity. Although in some cases the response was favorable, other comments were non-committal or negative. These are extracts from a study (*An Economic Review of the Patent System*) made for the committee in 1958 by Professor Fritz Machlup:

> No economist, on the basis of present knowledge, could possibly state with certainty that the patent system, as it now operates, confers a net benefit or a net loss upon society. The best he can do is to state assumptions and make guesses about the extent to which reality corresponds to assumptions.
>
> If we did not have a patent system, it would be irresponsible, on the basis of our present knowledge of its economic consequences, to recommend instituting one. But since we have had a patent system for a long time, it would be irresponsible, on the basis of our present knowledge, to recommend abolishing it.

In his study *The Impact of the Patent System on Research*, Professor Seymour Melman reached this conclusion:

> The patent system has lost the effectiveness that it may once have had as a way of promoting science and the useful arts. This has been owing to changes in the ways of producing knowledge, and to the damaging effects that competitive patenting activity has had upon the conduct of inquiry and research.

Professor Corwin D. Edwards, asked for his opinion on the economic aspects, gave this answer:

> The question whether on balance, our patent system accelerates or retards the rate at which inventions come into use requires comparison of any stimulating effect that it may have upon the rate of invention with any retarding effect that the exclusive

rights which it conveys may have, in spite of their mitigation by licensing and pooling. Since I believe that the stimulating effect has become slight and is most obvious where the purpose to keep the invention out of use is clear, I think that on balance the rate of application of new technology is retarded by our patent system.

The Senate subcommittee was not dismayed. In its 1965 report quoting the economists, it voiced these conclusions:

1. The objectives of the patent system are as valid today as at its inception.
2. The patent system has made a significant contribution to the technological progress and economic growth of this Nation. While the incentive afforded by the grant of a temporary monopoly continues to provide a stimulant for undertaking research, the nature of scientific research has greatly changed since the patent system was established. This alteration must be considered in appraising the contemporary role of the patent system.
3. There has not been adequate adjustment of our patent laws and procedures to reflect changing conditions and to respond to the critical problems confronting the Patent Office. The subcommittee is gratified at the efforts currently being undertaken in this direction by the Patent Office.
4. There is no justification for instituting fundamental changes in procedures merely for the sake of novelty or innovation. Proposals for change should be judged by whether they will strengthen the incentive to invent and also contribute to prompt disclosure of the invention to the public. The subcommittee also believes that it is not prudent to regard a single remedy, whether it be deferred examination, mechanized searching, or a larger Patent Office budget, as a talisman which will solve all the maladies of the patent system.

Many of the Senate subcommittee's publications are of value to students and historians of the patent system. The thirty studies mentioned earlier in this chapter, made by outside specialists, by members of the Library of Congress Legislative Reference Service, and by staff members of other agencies, include proposals for improving the patent system, efforts to establish a statutory standard of invention, discussions of compulsory licensing, economic aspects of the patent system, and practices abroad. Copies of many of the titles listed in the Bibliography at the end of this volume are still available. An additional 250-page report by Dr. S. C. Gilfillan, entitled "Invention and the Patent System," made originally for the Senate subcommittee, was published in 1964 by the Joint Economic Committee of Congress.

The Senate subcommittee follows closely the administration of the Patent Office, and its recommendations have weight on matters not requiring legislation. The group has encouraged the adoption of in-office steps designed to reduce the Patent Office burden, to speed examination, and to improve the quality of patents.

Close Watch on the Money

In the House of Representatives, funds for the Patent Office fall within the jurisdiction of an appropriations subcommittee for the departments of State, Justice, and Commerce, for the judiciary, and for related agencies. The chairman at this writing is Representative John J. Rooney of New York, not a man to mince words. At hearings in March, 1968, covering appropriations for fiscal 1969, Mr. Rooney examined Edward J. Brenner, Commissioner of Patents, who was accompanied by William F. Vier, director of the Patent Office Budget and Finance Division. Part of the record follows:

> MR. ROONEY. You have become quite ambitious. I understand that you went to the Secretary of Commerce and asked how much for the Patent Office?
> MR. BRENNER. We requested $48,209,000.
> MR. ROONEY. As compared to how much that you presently have?

MR. BRENNER. Presently requesting $42,742,000.

MR. ROONEY. Presently have?

MR. BRENNER. Presently have $38,200,000 in our 1968 appropriation.

MR. ROONEY. A mere $10 million increase?

MR. BRENNER. Yes, sir. Part of it was to take into account higher salary increases in the Government.

MR. ROONEY. That is a small part of it, isn't it, Commissioner?

MR. BRENNER. Yes. . . . I was going to add that the bulk of the additional money that we were asking from the Secretary was in the areas of modernization and mechanization.

MR. ROONEY. Now that is interesting. . . . One of the principal reasons for the Congress' support of the Research and Development Division was that you would come up with a method of searching prior patents by the use of a computer or machine. Is that so?

MR. BRENNER. That is correct. I am happy to say that we are making considerable progress at the present time to bringing in mechanized search systems.

MR. ROONEY. Commissioner, how many patents can now be searched by machine?

MR. BRENNER. It is in the range of about 1 percent at the present time.

MR. ROONEY. One percent?

MR. BRENNER. Yes, sir.

MR. ROONEY. In other words, it is negligible?

MR. BRENNER. It is a small factor at the present time but we are now starting to bring into implementation relatively large numbers of systems. We expect that this will increase significantly in the future. It is a major operation because there are over 15 million patent documents in our files. This takes considerable effort to convert to a mechanized search system.

MR. ROONEY. How many patents would you say can now be searched by machine so that we get the proper perspective?

MR. BRENNER. I would guess in the order of magnitude of about 100,000. . . .

MR. ROONEY. How many patents have been added to this machine each year for the last 5 years?

MR. BRENNER. In the past 5 years we have been primarily engaged in developing the tools and the procedures—

MR. ROONEY. Have any patents been added to this machine each year for the last 5 years?

MR. VIER. The steroid file has been continually updated. This is one of the machine systems.

MR. BRENNER. That is right. We are just now bringing on some systems in other areas.

MR. ROONEY. After these 10 years of expenditures, isn't it the fact that only a few thousand out of a total of over 3 million can now be searched by machine?

MR. BRENNER. Yes, sir. I believe in general that is a correct statement.

MR. ROONEY. Would you agree that we have wasted a lot of money over that 10 years?

MR. BRENNER. No, sir. I would respectfully like to say that most of the effort has gone into the development of the procedures and the techniques that would be used as well as to develop cooperative efforts with other countries. Now, the tools and the procedures are established—

MR. ROONEY. We are not talking about other countries. We are talking about our country, our money and our Patent Office and our attempts to do this work by machine or computer. Apparently we have been a colossal failure; would that be a fair statement?

MR. BRENNER. Well, sir, I would say that in any new type of system where it is necessary to do research and development, it is necessary to spend money to do research before you develop—

MR. ROONEY. Commissioner, all through this we are talking about 10 years of money, taxpayers' money spent for research and development for this purpose. The Patent Office now gives away quite a few patents to U.S. inventors and attorneys which could be sold for 50 cents or more apiece; is that a fact?

MR. BRENNER. Yes, sir. By statute, copies of U.S. patents cost 50 cents.

MR. ROONEY. How many thousands has the Patent Office given away each year? Take the last year, if you want to.

Mr. Brenner. Well, sir, as far as I know we have not given away copies of U.S. patents. We have charged the statutory fee of 50 cents.

Mr. Vier. They are only given away in order to facilitate the—

Mr. Rooney. Are they given away or sold for 50 cents, which is it? You say they are given away and the Commissioner says they are not given away, they are sold for 50 cents. Which is it?

Mr. Brenner. The copies of patents we sell to the general public we charge 50 cents for each patent copy. We do supply—

Mr. Rooney. I started on the subject of how many you give away. How many patents do you give away to the U.S. inventors and attorneys which could be sold for 50 cents? In other words, how many do you give away that you don't get 50 cents for?

Mr. Brenner. We supply complete sets of U.S. patents to 22 public libraries throughout the country.

Mr. Rooney. I am not asking about that, I am trying to get a figure on how many you give away, how many thousand.

Mr. Vier. About 1.7 million currently to applicants and examiners.

Mr. Brenner. With reference to—

Mr. Rooney. I have a distinct idea that you have a substantial operation over there requiring a batch of employees just to give away these patents.

Mr. Brenner. Well, sir, you must have reference to our program for supplying copies of references with our Office actions to patent applicants. These we do not charge any special fee for. This is provided for by the statute which authorizes the Commissioner to—

Mr. Rooney. I am not suggesting there is anything illegal about giving these away. I am merely trying to find out how many you are giving away.

The next hearings, on appropriations for fiscal 1970, were held in May, 1969, a few days after William E. Schuyler, Jr., had been sworn in as the new Commissioner. "You get a brass ring," said Mr. Rooney, "since this is your first appearance."

After Mr. Schuyler read a prepared statement, the colloquy began:

MR. ROONEY. Mr. Schuyler, at page 5 of your statement, the last sentence on that page, you say: "We have experienced greater overhead costs due to the new physical location of the Patent Office." Will you please elaborate on that?

MR. SCHUYLER. Those costs, Mr. Chairman, are mainly increased telephone charges, which I understand are based on higher rates at the new location, and the need to provide additional guard service because of the nature of the buildings in which the patent documents are contained.

MR. ROONEY. Can anybody accompanying Mr. Schuyler tell us whether or not these things were taken into consideration when the move was made?

MR. VIER. At the time the contract was signed with the General Services Administration—

MR. ROONEY. What contract?

MR. VIER. For space and services for the Patent Office personnel. No, sir. They have a telephone switchboard within the area at Crystal Plaza.

MR. ROONEY. When you say "no, sir" what do you mean? I cannot follow you.

MR. VIER. This is within the metropolitan area.

MR. ROONEY. What is?

MR. VIER. Crystal Plaza, and it was not anticipated that the rates would be any higher over there for the Government than it would be in any other place within the metropolitan area. They do run higher.

MR. ROONEY. I guess when you said "no" and I did not know what you meant at that particular point, I should take it "no" means you did not anticipate increased telephone and guard rates of almost $100,000 at the time the move was being considered?

MR. VIER. Yes, sir, that is correct.

Mr. Vier carried most of the burden during the hearing,

in which Representative Elford A. Cederberg of Michigan asked a few questions. When Mr. Rooney did not understand a figure of $2.5 million, he returned to Mr. Schuyler.

MR. ROONEY. Now I still don't know how this got up to $2.5 million after that testimony; do you, Mr. Schuyler? . . .

MR. SCHUYLER. It is my understanding that the amount in the Patent Office budget covered only a part of the space during the first year of occupancy of that space; that the $2.5 million is involved in the 10-year contract which Mr. Cederberg mentioned. That remains with the General Services Administration. The smaller amounts that appear in the Patent Office budget were for the Patent Office to pay their share of the first year of any rental of new space. I am not sure that is a clear explanation but that is my understanding of it.

MR. ROONEY. It is not clear enough for me. This is about as ridiculous a move as I have ever seen in all my years in the Government. Ridiculous. I don't know what to say about this. In 20 plus years I have heard about all the plans and how the Patent Office Commissioners were going to streamline things, that everything was going to come out right. Here it is 23 years later and it has never happened. So I wish you luck.

MR. SCHUYLER. Thank you, sir.

MR. ROONEY. Very well, thank you, gentlemen.

MR. SCHUYLER. Thank you, Mr. Chairman.

In the hearings, Mr. Rooney was talking about money requested by the Patent Office from the Secretary of Commerce in the first of several steps toward getting appropriations. With successive parings, such requests go from Commerce to budget officials in the White House, and then, in a Presidential message, to Congress. The step procedure is not unique but common to most agencies. "Everybody whacks at it," said one Patent Office official. In conference, sometimes the Senate has added a little to what the House proposed for the Patent Office. The over-all results show progress. The appropriation for fiscal 1961 was just under $24 million, and that for 1971 is $52.2 million.

IX

The Patent Office and the Public

The Patent Office has several publics: the lawyers and inventors with whom it does business directly, the corporation executives and technologists who use it as a research center, and the vast general citizenry.

The immediate public is rather substantial. The PTC Research Institute of George Washington University has estimated the number of living inventors at 385,000, of whom 160,000 are employed and 225,000 are independents. About 25 per cent of patents are issued to individual inventors, 5 per cent to government and university personnel, and 70 per cent to corporations (of which about half go to small companies). Contacts with inventors and their employers are chiefly through patent attorneys and agents. There are 9,400 of these.

The American who has never invented anything or acquired a financial interest in an invention has a vaguely favorable impression of the patent system and the machinery provided by the Patent Office but as a rule is innocent of any specific knowledge about them. Among the things that astonish the layman are the volume, variety, and detail of patents. On Tuesday March 10, 1970, the 3.5 *millionth* U.S. patent was issued. During every week of 1969 and early 1970, exactly 1,300 patents were granted, not counting design and plant patents, and more could have been issued if the budget had permitted. Titles included: Device for Determining the Soot Content of Flue Gases; Archimedean Screw Pump; Electronic Device for Automatic Indication, Registration and Forecast of Local and Distant Thunderstorms; and Monoazo Compounds Containing a Piperazine Type Ring Substituted by an Organo Sulfonyl Group.

One popular assumption is that if a product is patented you can go to a store and buy it. But a patented process or article may be entirely conceptual, existing only in the discoverer's mind and in the drawings and description. A reporter once asked the patentee of a flying saucer whether he had built one. The inventor answered that the question was foolish, because, of course, he didn't have the million dollars. Another misapprehension is that the Russians steal American patents. Actually the two governments exchange copies of patents they issue. Any resident of the Soviet Union is perfectly free to use what he finds in a U.S. patent unless the invention is also patented in the U.S.S.R. A patent valid both in this country and abroad is still a dream.

Fortunately the impression, once rather general, that all inventors are screwballs but that if one patents a better mousetrap the world will beat a path to his door, is dying out. It is pretty widely recognized that many inventors are engineers or scientists and that new mousetraps require salesmanship.

PUBLICATIONS

Anybody who wants to find out about the Patent Office itself can do so readily without going to Washington. (If he does go to the District of Columbia, of course, he will find that the Patent Office is not there but in a suburban development called Crystal Plaza in nearby Arlington County, Virginia.) A series of simple booklets, published by the agency's Office of Information Services, is available by mail. Single copies are free, and larger quantities may be ordered from the Superintendent of Documents, Government Printing Office, Washington D.C., 20402. An excellent primer is *General Information Concerning Patents*, which summarizes the workings of the Patent Office, tells what applicants must do, lists fees, and defines patents, trademarks, and copyrights. *Patents and Inventions: An Information Aid for Inventors* supplements *General Information* and gives a step-by-step procedure for the inventor, as well as some advice on marketing. Other booklets in the series are listed in the Bibliography at the end of this volume. They include a history, *The Story of the United States Patent Office*, and answers to the most commonly asked questions about patents, trademarks, and plant patents.

In addition to the Patent Office booklets, the Department of Commerce has published *Patents: Spur to American Progress*, which discusses the value and development of the American patent system, its relations to business, and patenting abroad. The Patent Office also provides a valuable set of guides for the professional (listed by title under "Government Publications" in the Bibliography). Among those useful both to lawyers and examiners are *Patent Laws, Manual of Classification, Rules of Practice of the United States Patent Office in Patent Cases, Trademark Rules of Practice, Manual of Patent Examining Procedure*, and the annual *Decisions of the Commissioner of Patents*. For the student and independent inventor there are the *Commissioner of Patents Annual Report* and the booklets mentioned above.

The most important publications, however, are copies of patents themselves, which may be ordered by mail from the Commissioner of Patents, Washington, D.C., 20231, at 50 cents each (20 cents for trademarks and designs and $1 for plant patents). Microfilmed copies of complete patents, beginning in 1966, are available on subscription from the National Technical Information Service, Springfield, Virginia, 22151. Microfilmed lists of patent numbers, by subclass, are available from the same source.

Patents do not trickle out on the five days of the business week but are issued in a minor flood every Tuesday. Even if Tuesday happens to be Christmas, the patents and the *Official Gazette* that lists and abstracts them are published as of 12 o'clock noon. On business Tuesdays, promptly at midday, the *Official Gazette* of the Patent Office is placed on sale at Government Printing Office bookstores.* This useful booksize publication lists all the patents of the week, with a brief abstract of each and one drawing, if there are drawings. It also carries official announcements, "defensive publications," court decisions, and trademark notices. It is kept on file in more than four hundred libraries throughout the United States and is available on a subscription basis from the Government Printing Office. Copies of patents themselves are to be found, filed in numerical order, in libraries in the following cities:

Albany, New York *(University of the State of New York Library)*
Atlanta, Georgia *(Georgia Tech Library)*
Boston, Massachusetts *(Public Library)*
Buffalo, New York *(Public Library)*
Chicago, Illinois *(Public Library)*
Cincinnati, Ohio *(Public Library)*

---

* In 1970, for the first time in twenty-five years, a fortnight passed without the issuance of any patents for inventions. A wage dispute in the Government Printing Office forced the Patent Office to grant only reissued (corrected) patents, design patents, and trademark registrations on June 9 and 16. The *Official Gazette* for those two weeks was a slim booklet instead of the usual thick volume. Two weeks were skipped in 1945 in compliance with then existing law, because of a temporary vacancy in the office of Commissioner of Patents. Otherwise patents have been issued every week since 1848, and for more than a century Tuesday has been the customary day.

Cleveland, Ohio *(Public Library)*
Columbus, Ohio *(Ohio State University Library)*
Detroit, Michigan *(Public Library)*
Kansas City, Missouri *(Linda Hall Library)*
Los Angeles, California *(Public Library)*
Madison, Wisconsin *(State Historical Society Library)*
Milwaukee, Wisconsin *(Public Library)*
New York City *(Public Library)*
Newark, New Jersey *(Public Library)*
Philadelphia, Pennsylvania *(Franklin Institute Library)*
Pittsburgh, Pennsylvania *(Carnegie Library)*
Providence, Rhode Island *(Public Library)*
St. Louis, Missouri *(Public Library)*
Stillwater, Oklahoma *(Oklahoma A&M College Library)*
Sunnyvale, California *(Public Library)*
Toledo, Ohio *(Public Library)*

The Sunnyvale library has arranged its collection, dating from January 2, 1962, by subject matter. Some of the above libraries maintain microfilmed lists of patents by subclass, so that a researcher can find those in his field of interest. Lists of patent numbers in given classes and subclasses can also be obtained from the Patent Office.

INFORMATION SERVICES

The Patent Office provides a reservoir of technology that industry can tap. Aside from the searches conducted to find out whether something can be patented, executives use the Public Search Room in Crystal City and buy patent copies to determine the "state of the art" before embarking on a new project. The head of a new product division, for instance, wants to know what his company's competitors have done already. A technologist wants to avoid duplicating others' experiments and studies. As a Patent Office official put it, they want to be sure that they are not building a road that someone else has already paved.

The number of industrial visitors to the Public Search Room is known to be substantial, but no nose count is kept. Many visitors to the Patent Office, including students and children, start with the Office of Information Services. A boy of eight or nine, accompanied by his mother and sister, may inquire about patenting a toy automobile. He will be given some booklets and sent to the Search Room.

The Office of Information Services is a small unit with a good many jobs. Its director advises the Commissioner of Patents on public relations policies and on the dissemination of information about the Patent Office to its several publics. Like information spokesmen throughout government, he is expected to put his agency's best foot forward. Isaac Fleischmann, who formerly ran the Patent Office Training Branch and served as assistant to the Commissioner of Patents on special projects, has headed the Office of Information Services since it was created in 1958. He is popular with the working press and has received the Silver Anvil Award from the Public Relations Society of America.

Besides organizing press conferences for the Commissioner of Patents in the home office and in many cities, the duties of the director and his two assistants include

- Preparing the Commissioner's annual reports, the printed rosters of attorneys, and the information booklets already mentioned
- Maintaining contacts with the Patent, Trademark, and Copyright Law Section of the American Bar Association, with the American Patent Law Association, and with more than forty local groups
- Providing speakers from the Patent Office staff for universities, scientific and other societies, and state inventors' exhibitions. Displays are often furnished. (From fifty to seventy-five addresses are arranged each year for college audiences alone. The Patent Office participates in the International Science Fair held by Science Service, and an annual briefing for col-

lege and university science and engineering faculty members and students is held at Crystal Plaza.)

- Staging an annual "Progress of Industry through Patents" exhibit at the Patent Office, in which 15-20 major corporations provide displays (Five hundred companies have participated since 1954.)
- Supplying information and cooperation to the press associations, newspapers, general magazines, the trade and technical press, and radio and television stations and networks

The press work is probably the most important function of the Office of Information Services. Besides distributing news releases on general matters, the section encourages publications to carry stories on individual patents as they are issued. The *New York Times* publishes each Saturday a "Patents of the Week" column, describing inventions of general interest patented on the preceding Tuesday, a feature distributed to many other newspapers in the United States and abroad by the New York Times News Service.

To make it possible for correspondents to trace patents originating in their areas, the *Official Gazette* now includes a geographical index of inventors, with which a reporter can find out who in his home town invented what. If the abstract does not tell him enough, he can get a full copy of the patent. The geographical index has proved to be handy for congressmen and for state planning and development commissions. A number of congressmen tell about their constituents' patents in their regular newsletters. The Office of Information Services sends a list of District of Columbia, Maryland, and Virginia inventors each week to the local press.

Writers for the technical magazines can trace current patents in their fields by checking the "Classification of Patents" table in the *Official Gazette*. A score of publications carry weekly or monthly columns covering inventions of specific interest to their readerships, sometimes reproducing drawings. Among these publications are *Modern Knitting*

Management, Computers and Automation, Pulp and Paper, Textile Bulletin, Machine Design, Foundry Monthly, Engineering and Mining Journal, Food Engineering, and *Modern Plastics. Science Digest* features a patent each month. *Science News* carries occasional articles on news of the patent system. For small-arms sportsmen, *The American Rifleman* publishes a monthly list. Among the Washington technical letters that give news of recent patents are *Space Propulsion* and *Radioisotope Report.*

The Office of Information Services calls the attention of publications to the availability of patent news in their fields but does not select specific patents as important. The writer must make his own choice. Patent owners often send out news releases and advance tips on patents about to be issued, since the number and issue date of each are known by the attorneys weeks in advance.

The writer for newspapers recognizes that each trade or profession writes and talks in its own idiom. He must translate the patent news into language that the general reader will understand. One approach that has often proved useful is to ask a technical spokesman, "How would you explain this to your sister-in-law from Ohio, who has never been in your shop?"

THE MAIL ROOM

The Office of Information Services of the Patent Office handles correspondence with the media and with such inquirers as teachers who want material for their classes and students preparing theses, but the principal burden of about 2.5 million pieces of mail each year falls on the agency's mail room. Between 80,000 and 90,000 envelopes are received each month. The bulk comes from patent attorneys who may enclose an average of four papers in each, intended for different sections of the agency.

Most of the routine questions, such as how to obtain a patent or register a trademark, are answered with copies of the information booklets. Letters arrive from all over the world, in many languages, and from all kinds of people. Some are neatly typed; others are handwritten, with hand-drawn illustrations; many are virtually illegible. The subjects range from intellectual property to bombs. Now and then a clearly lettered communication, with perfect spelling and syntax, conveys no practical meaning. The mail room has a "crank file" of letters that there is no use answering because they repeat questions that have been answered in earlier replies to the same people. One Maine correspondent labeled a 1969 communication "My 94th letter concerning patent and copyright legislation."

PRIVATE ORGANIZATIONS

Several membership organizations constitute an important segment of the Patent Office's "public." The Patent, Trademark, and Copyright Law Section of the American Bar Association and the American Patent Law Association, another organization of patent lawyers, play important roles in patent legislation. Their activities in this connection will be discussed in Chapter X.

In addition to the bar associations, there are a number of private organizations concerned with patents and other intellectual property. One is the PTC Research Institute of George Washington University, Washington, D.C. As the initials in its name imply, the institute conducts studies in patents, trademarks, and copyrights of the United States and foreign countries and disseminates information about them. The institute holds conferences in Washington and regional meetings in various cities, makes an annual Charles F. Kettering award for meritorious work in the field, and names an annual "inventor of the year." Its publications include papers, educational booklets, and the journal *IDEA*, published five times a year. Members receive guides to the institute's research, digests, news notes, bulletins, and reports. Of interest to young people is a series of booklets with such titles as *The Patent System All Around You; The Trademark: The Maker's Monogram;* and *The "C" in the Circle.*

The history of the institute goes back to February 15, 1949, when the American Patent Law Association, by resolution later ratified in a referendum, recognized a need for research and education under university auspices in the patent and related systems. An office was opened in the university's law school the following year, and the institute celebrated its twentieth anniversary in 1970. In the same year it was announced that the institute would become independent of the university not later than June 30, 1972.

Research has been aimed at the interests of the industrial and private patent owner, the inventor, the patent lawyer, and the student. Recent studies made by staff and outside investigators have analyzed the recommendations of the President's Commission on the Patent System, pending international treaties and conventions, computer software protection, and other current problems. The membership includes corporations and individuals throughout the United States and in more than thirty countries abroad.

The Patent Office Society, founded in 1917, is "dedicated to promotion of the patent and trademark systems and the fostering of a true appreciation thereof." The membership, which is limited to present and former professional staff members of the Patent Office, registered patent attorneys and agents in private practice or with federal agencies, and federal judges, approached 1,500 in 1970. Besides social programs for members and their families, the society holds meetings at which legislative and policy questions are discussed. The organization is best known for the monthly *Journal of the Patent Office Society*, a leading source of research material. *Journal* subscribers include libraries and technical societies around the world. The magazine describes itself as "a medium of expression for the exchange of thought in the fields of patents, trademarks and copyrights; a forum for the presentation and discussion of legal and technical subjects relating to the useful arts; a periodical for the dissemination of knowledge of the functional attributes of the patent, trademark, and copyright laws, in order to effect a more uniform practice thereof and through which all interested in the development thereof may work to a common end."

The National Patent Council, Inc., a nonprofit organization with headquarters in Washington, is a spokesman for small businessmen, attorneys, and inventors. Founded in 1945 by the late John Will Anderson of Gary, Indiana, an inventor and manufacturer, the council in 1970 had about 400 individual and 100 corporate members and was affiliated with the National Small Business Association, which had a reported membership of 35,000. The two organizations were consolidating forces on legislative issues. The expressed purpose of the council is to promote a broader public understanding and appreciation of the American patent system and to defend and explain its essentials. The council's outspoken monthly newsletter, *Patent Trends*, reports on proposed Patent Office procedures and laws and on the rights of patent owners. Both the council and its executive vice-president have registered as lobbyists with Congress.

There are a number of inventors' associations, mostly organized on a regional basis. One California group offered to each charter sponsor who made a contribution of $25 or more a special honorary Doctor of Development degree. In 1969, private collections of old patent models, such as were required with applications until about 1880, were offered for display by Ideas, Ingenuity and Inventions in America, Inc., a company formed in Dallas, Texas, by Robert M. Sinks, Jack R. Crosby, and Fred Lieberman. One such exhibition, put on in

New York by the furniture division of U.S. Plywood-Champion Papers, Inc., included a miniature working model of a wardrobe-bed, patented in 1864 by F. Cotton. The Dallas company planned to open patent-model galleries around the country.

Although patent models are now museum pieces, each household has its own collection of inventions. Many articles in the kitchen, living room, and even the hall closet—can-openers, clocks, lamps, telephones, coat-hangers, or whatever—represent temporary monopolies, expired or still in force, awarded to their inventors by a grateful society. Everybody, whether consciously or not, is a patron of the patent system.

X

Controversies

Patents represent a limited monopoly, so it is not surprising that many of them have led to disputes. A hundred years ago, as we have seen in Chapter IV, American dentists resented paying royalties for the right to use hard rubber in making false teeth plates, and one of them settled the matter out of court by shooting the patent owner. Since that time there have been legislative attempts to limit the patent monopoly through forms of compulsory licensing and to claim for the public all rights to patents obtained through federal financing. The most recent controversy arose over the recommendations of a federal commission to make it easier to patent abroad by giving the American system a foreign shape. A much-watered "patent reform" bill is still pending.

Inventors have long poured into attentive congressional ears general complaints: that patents take too long to get and cost too much; that they are expensive to defend in law suits; and that too many of them are invalidated when they get into court. The reduction in time and costs and improvement in patent quality were among the objectives of the President's Commission on the Patent System, expressed in its report published in 1966 and followed shortly by an Administration bill, offered to carry the recommendations into effect. Another objective was "to make U.S. patent practice more compatible with that of other major countries, wherever consistent with the objectives of the U.S. patent system."

"FIRST TO FILE"

The commission's chief concession to foreign practice, and the one that aroused widest opposition, was urging American adoption of the "first to file" system common abroad. The traditional procedure in the United States has been to recognize, between rival claimants, the inventor who can prove he was the first to invent. The only other countries that follow similar procedure are Canada and the Philippines. The commission's report stated:

> In a first to file system the respective dates of "conception" and "reduction to practice" of the invention, presently of great importance in resolving contested priority for an invention claimed in two or more pending applications or patents, no longer would be considered. Instead, the earliest effective filing date would determine the question of priority.

The Patent Office was directly involved in the ensuing controversy. Edward J. Brenner, then Commissioner of Patents, appeared with Department of Commerce officials and members of the presidential commission before congressional committees in support of the bill.

Opposition to the proposed law was voiced by individual attorneys and inventors as harmful to the little fellow (the lone inventor and garage entrepreneur). When the bar associations got through with their committee work, they entered formal objections to two provisions. One was the "first to file" section. The other was the plan to abandon the "year of grace," the period allowed an inventor after public use, sale, or publication of his invention before he must apply for a patent. The year gives him time for development and market tests.

Robert W. Fulwider of Los Angeles, chairman of the Patent, Trademark and Copyright Law Section of the American Bar Association, told a Senate committee that the first to file proposal was tantamount to a repudiation of the philosophy of rewarding the first to invent, to which the United States had been firmly committed since 1836. His section's disapproval of the two provisions was later ratified by the association's governing body, the House of Delegates. The American Patent Law Association, the other national organization of patent lawyers, took a similar stand against the two provisions.

The American Bar Association prepared its own bill, which was introduced in the Senate. In the 1969 session, after conferring with William E. Schuyler, Jr., the new Commissioner of Patents, Senator John L. McClellan, chairman of the Subcommittee on Patents, Trademarks, and Copyrights of the Senate Judiciary Committee, introduced a bill on which he hoped there would be a meeting of minds. An identical bill was introduced in the House. The McClellan bill retained both the first to invent policy and the year of grace. If, after House action (expected by 1971), it is adopted, the principal changes from the present law (Title 35) will be these:

1. Nominal acceptance is given to the first to file principle by a provision that whenever the same invention is claimed in two applications, the patent is to be issued on the one with the earlier U.S. filing date. However, in a priority contest (interference), another applicant who proves earlier invention will be recognized.
2. The term of a patent will be twenty years from the date the application is filed, instead of seventeen years from the date of the patent's issuance.
3. Anyone can have a patent re-examined by submitting within six months of its issuance a list of publications and earlier patents with an explanation of their bearing on the unpatent-

ability of the claims in the questioned patent. If finally found unpatentable, the claims will be considered canceled. Under present law, the Patent Office has no jurisdiction for re-examination once a patent is granted, and validity can only be attacked in court.

4. A patent application may be filed by the assignee or the inventor, provided the latter gives later clearance. Under present law the inventor must sign and file the application except in very special circumstances.

In the McClellan bill an effort has been made to raise the standard of patentability that the Patent Office must apply. The agency is also required to recover at least 65 per cent of operating costs through fees and to recommend changes to Congress if the receipts fall below that percentage.

Among the recommendations of the President's Commission that have been ignored are: inclusion of foreign knowledge, use, and sale as "prior art"; preliminary applications and deferred examination; elimination of design and plant patents; and appointment of civil commissioners and an advisory council. Spokesmen for industry have expressed regret at the elimination of Recommendation No. XXII, which was aimed at clarifying the licensable nature of the rights granted by patents, and have blamed the Department of Justice for its removal.

TNEC vs. National Patent Planning Commission

More than three decades ago the Temporary National Economic Committee (TNEC), whose membership represented both Congress and the executive branch, stirred the country with its investigation of the concentration of economic power. It also stirred the usually placid patent community with its charges and recommendations.

The committee was established by joint congressional resolution in 1938, after receipt of a message from President Franklin D. Roosevelt recommending, among other things, amendment of the patent laws "to prevent their use to suppress inventions, and to create industrial monopolies. Of course," the message continued, "such amendment should not deprive the inventor of his royalty rights, but, generally speaking, future patents might be made available for use by anyone upon payment of appropriate royalties. Open patent pools have voluntarily been put into effect in a number of important industries with wholesome results."

In its final report, issued March 31, 1941, after expending more than $1 million in appropriations, the committee declared that the privilege accorded by the patent monopoly had been shamefully abused and "used as a device to control whole industries, to suppress competition, to restrict output, to enhance prices, to suppress inventions, and to discourage inventiveness." The same report cited foreign patent controls over American industry. The interchange of patents between American and foreign concerns was said to have been used as a means of cartelizing industry so as to effectively displace competition.

The TNEC was particularly concerned at the effect of monopolistic practices on defense, since America was then threatened by what was to become World War II. "The production of vitally important materials, such as beryllium, magnesium, optical glass, and chemicals," said the report, "has been restrained through international patent controls and cross-licensing, which have divided the world market into closed areas." The most striking recommendations were for laws to restrict licensing and to limit suits for infringement. The report of the committee said:

> We recommend that the Congress enact legislation which will require that any future patent is to be available for use by anyone who may desire its use and who is willing to pay a fair price for the privilege. Machinery, either judicial or administrative, should be set up to determine whether the

royalty demanded by the patentee may fairly be said to represent reasonable compensation or is intended to set a prohibitive price for such use.

Licenses were to be unrestricted. The holder of a patent would not be permitted to restrict a licensee as to volume of production, price, use, or geographical area. Patent owners could be deprived of their rights if they violated the licensing restrictions. Any licensing agreement was to be recorded in writing and a copy was to be filed with the Federal Trade Commission.

A further TNEC recommendation was that "in order to prevent the use of litigation as a weapon of business aggression rather than as an instrument for adjudicating honest disputes," no infringement action be permitted against a licensee or purchaser of an article unless a judgment had previously been obtained against the licensor or manufacturer.

The TNEC licensing and infringement proposals have never become law. Two other less controversial patent reforms have been urged by other public bodies and may yet be adopted. One is for a single court of patent appeals and the other, which is virtually unopposed at present, is to change the patent term from seventeen years after issuance to twenty years after the application filing date. Several procedural changes that had been advocated by the TNEC in a preliminary 1939 report were enacted into law.

Orthodox believers in the patent system were particularly shocked by TNEC Monograph 31, *Patents and Free Enterprise*, prepared for the committee by Walton Hamilton, professor of law at Yale University. In scholarly language, he painted a dark and hopeless picture. At law, he said, the patent was a letter which certified invention and rewarded the inventor. In fact, he continued, it had become an asset to business, a fence about the corporate estate, a weapon of competitive strategy for private industrial government. Professor Hamilton rejected the contention of persons who recited that under the prevailing system technology had taken giant strides and who insisted that the patent grant was the cause. "The plain truth is," he wrote, "that a complete revision of the patent system is long overdue."

On December 12, 1941, a few days after Pearl Harbor, President Roosevelt appointed a National Patent Planning Commission, with five distinguished members. The chairman was Charles F. Kettering, inventor of the self-starter and other automotive devices; Chester C. Davis, president of the Federal Reserve Bank of St. Louis; Francis P. Gaines, president of Washington and Lee University; Edward F. McGrady, head of labor relations for RCA; and Owen D. Young, honorary chairman of the General Electric Company.

The commission published three reports, none of them really controversial. In the first, issued June 19, 1943, it called the patent system the foundation of American enterprise, which had demonstrated its value over a period coextensive with the life of the government. "The principle of recognizing a property right in intellectual creation," said the commission, "is sound and should be continued as contemplated in the Constitution."

Several changes in the patent laws were recommended. One was the recording of all patent agreements with the Patent Office. Another was that in an infringement suit the patent owner be limited to reasonable compensation without prohibiting the use of the invention whenever the court found its manufacture necessary to national defense or required by public health or public safety. The commission also recommended a public register in the Patent Office of patents available for license. Such a register is now maintained.

To provide a yardstick as to what constitutes invention, the commission proposed that Congress declare a national standard "whereby patentability of an invention shall be determined by the objective test as to its advancement of the arts and sciences." In an infringement suit, the court would refer the record to the Patent Office for its opinion.

Two reforms urged by the commission have been incorporated in the pending patent bill: limitation of the patent term to twenty years from the application filing date, and opportunity for any member of the public to challenge the validity of any patent within six months after its grant.

The final proposal in the first report was that the Court of Customs and Patent Appeals be designated as the sole reviewing body upon the denial of a patent by the Patent Office. The second report, issued in 1944, made general observations on policies concerning government-owned patents, those resulting from federally financed research, and those issued to federal employees. Some years later President Truman set policies on employee inventors, and President Kennedy on inventions made with federal funds.

In its third and final report, submitted in June, 1945, the commission rejected "those proposals for revision of our patent system involving a departure from the principles upon which it is founded and by the effectuation of which it has furthered the nation's industrial and social improvement." Specifically, it declined to accept the idea of the general compulsory licensing of patents, as such a change would endanger small enterprises.

The commission's mild reforms can hardly have satisfied Professor Hamilton.

THE QUESTION OF INDEPENDENCE

The Patent Office has always been part of a Cabinet department. It was a unit in the Department of State until 1849, when it was transferred to the Department of the Interior. In 1925 it was shifted to the Department of Commerce, where it remains.

For a century and a half, opinion has been divided as to whether inclusion of this agency in a department is good or bad. On the one hand, it is possible for the agency to get the President's attention through Cabinet representation. On the other hand, there is the fear of interference in quasi-judicial matters by department officers with political interests and a lack of professional knowledge.

Since the Patent Office was established, several bills have been introduced in Congress with the object of making the organization an independent agency. The movement is still very much alive. The Patent, Trademark, and Copyright Law Section of the American Bar Association adopted a resolution in August, 1968, approving in principle "the establishment of the Patent Office as an independent agency in the executive branch of the government." The matter has not, at this writing, been presented to the House of Delegates, the association's governing body, nor has the American Patent Law Association, the other influential bar association in the field, taken any recent action.

A prominent advocate of independence is Robert C. Watson, a Washington patent lawyer who was Commissioner of Patents during the eight years of the Eisenhower Administration. In the *Journal of the Patent Office Society* for March, 1968, Mr. Watson cited these actions favoring independence:

1812—Report of House of Representatives special committee
1884—Bill by Senator O. H. Platt of Connecticut
1912—Bill by Representative William A. Oldfield, supported by Edward B. Moore, Commissioner of Patents
1912—Report of the President's Commission on Economy and Efficiency
1919—Report of the National Research Council
1919—House of Representatives bill
1957—Bill by Senators Joseph C. O'Mahoney and Alexander Wiley
1959—Bill by the same sponsors

Early in 1959, a Senate subcommittee report had this to say about a staff study recommending that the Patent Office be made independent:

This staff report to the subcommittee concludes that the present subordination of the Patent Office to the Commerce Department is inconsistent with proper performance of the quasi-judicial functions involved in granting patents. When such a quasi-judicial agency is made subordinate to an executive department it is inevitably handicapped. The Patent Office will also be handicapped in discharging its administrative responsibilities so long as Congress must rely upon the Secretary of Commerce, rather than on the Commissioner of Patents, to present proposals needed to remedy deficiencies in physical facilities and personnel. Illustrative of this latter problem is the fact that [the pay bill], which made possible a lifting of Patent Office salaries to a point commensurate with Patent Office responsibility, was opposed, insofar as it attempted to achieve this objective, by the Secretary of Commerce. There are also other deficiencies, repeatedly called to the attention of the Secretary of Commerce which the Secretary has never taken steps to correct.

The subcommittee staff concluded that the need for an independent patent office was established as long ago as 1912 when the President's Commission on Economy and Efficiency recommended that it should be moved into a building of its own and that it should be an independent bureau subject only to the supervision of the President where supervision is needed. This conclusion has been endorsed and reiterated whenever an official investigation of this matter has been made. The report further states that the present emphasis on acceleration of our scientific research and development has made the work in the Patent Office increasingly critical. The subordination of the Patent Office to the executive branch of the Government was an historical accident which may have handicapped our technological progress in the past, and may continue to do so in the future unless the Office is given the independent status that its importance deserves.

Nine years before, in 1950, President Harry S. Truman had submitted Reorganization Plan No. 5 to Congress. The plan had drawn opposition from those who were against concentrating authority over Patent Office operations in the Secretary of Commerce. The plan, which was to go into effect within sixty days unless rejected by either house of Congress, provided that, with certain exceptions (not including the Patent Office) "there are hereby transferred to the Secretary of Commerce all functions of all other officers of the Department of Commerce and all functions of all agencies and employees of such Department." The Secretary was also authorized to delegate such powers to others.

The American Patent Law Association adopted resolutions opposing the assumption of Patent Office powers. As its representative, Mr. Watson testified against the plan before a House committee. Others appeared before a Senate committee, but neither the Senate nor the House objected, and the plan became effective. In 1962, under authority of the plan, Luther H. Hodges, then Secretary of Commerce, delegated to the Assistant Secretary of Commerce for Science and Technology (a newly created post) authority to approve regulations issued by the Commissioner of Patents.

The first incumbent as Assistant Secretary for Science and Technology was Dr. J. Herbert Hollomon, who later became president of the University of Oklahoma. In a public address late in 1964, he undertook to explain his role with respect to the Patent Office. First, he said, the Commissioner of Patents was responsible for the operation of the patent system within the framework of existing laws, but the Secretary of Commerce had the over-all authority and responsibility for general management and policy. "After the establishment of my office," he continued, "the Secretary delegated to me the responsibility that he has always had, of general policy direction of the Patent Office and direct line responsibility of working with the Commissioner of Patents in matters having to do with policy direction."

In the 1968 magazine article cited above, Mr. Watson expressed the belief that the Secretary or his appointee could, if he so chose, decide individual cases arising in the Patent Office. So far as is known, there has been no recent attempt by any Secretary of Commerce or one of his associates to interfere with the right of the Commissioner of Patents to decide questions arising under the patent and trademark laws, but Mr. Watson believes that one of his predecessors was subjected to pressure from above in a case involving a question of patentability of an invention, and he wants to eliminate the possibility that this may happen in the future. (It was generally understood that Mr. Watson's successor, David L. Ladd, had resigned as Commissioner in 1963 in part as a protest at the department's intrusion into internal affairs of the Patent Office.)

On the question of making the Patent Office an independent agency, objections have been made that the federal government would be more efficient with fewer, rather than more, independent agencies and that such a move would create a clamor for others; that the Patent Office would lose Cabinet representation; and once it was independent might be swallowed by another department not as helpful as Commerce.

Mr. Watson's answer has been that Cabinet representation is unnecessary, as Patent Office affairs are dealt with by Congress. He regards the other two objections as based on pure speculation. In his opinion, making the agency independent would not increase operating costs.

PATENTING COMPUTER PROGRAMS

A recent controversy to which the Patent Office was a party involved the patenting of computer programs—called "software" to distinguish them from the electronic and mechanical computer "hardware." In October, 1968, the Patent Office published guidelines making it clear that it did not intend to grant patents for programs unless they were embodied in something mechanical. This policy had been followed for several years, during which programs were patented only if they were embodied in equipment, such as gears, cams, and electric circuits. Edward J. Brenner, Commissioner of Patents, said that if software should be made patentable the filing of thousands of additional applications would impose a tremendous burden on the Patent Office.

The protection of software, however, was of prime interest to the growing section of the computer industry producing it. A trade estimate was that there were 425 software firms in the country, as distinct from the concerns turning out the machines, or hardware, and the hundreds of data centers selling computer time. Four weeks after the Patent Office announcement, the U.S. Court of Customs and Patent Appeals, in what Chief Judge Eugene Worley called a landmark case, ruled that computer programs were patentable. Acting on a petition filed by the Patent Office, which suggested that the decision (in *Prater and Wei*) was making mental processes patentable and that such a patent could be infringed by somebody with pencil and paper, the court held a rehearing in March, 1969. A revised decision, handed down by the court the following August, was interpreted by lawyers as meaning that the operation of computers under the control of new programs was patentable. Programs themselves, in the form of punched cards or magnetic tape, remained unpatentable.

The software industry welcomed the decision. It expected to get patents on the operation of computers with its programs —something almost as good as patenting the programs themselves. In October, 1969, the new Commissioner of Patents, William E. Schuyler, Jr., rescinded the guidelines. The published notice added, "For the time being, adoption of new guidelines for the examination of patent applications is being deferred pending further judicial interpretation of the law on a case-by-case basis." By February, 1970, the Court of Customs and Patent Appeals had issued two additional decisions that were interpreted by lawyers as opening the Patent Office door a little wider to the protection of software. Means of protection other than patents are treated in Chapter VI.

PATENTS AND GOVERNMENT CONTRACTORS

A long-standing controversy involving patents, but not the Patent Office directly, has been over rights to inventions resulting from research and development work by contractors using federal funds. Contentions have ranged from government-take-all (on behalf of the public) to industry-take-all. In 1961 the late Senator Estes Kefauver of Tennessee introduced a bill providing, among other things, that owners of new drug patents must, after three years, grant their competitors licenses to make the products. Senator Russell B. Long of Louisiana introduced another bill that would require all federal agencies to take title to patents resulting from government-financed research.

The Kefauver bill was opposed by industry not only because of its expected effects on the drug business but because of its threat of future amendments to the patent law affecting other industries. Neither bill became law, nor have other proposals to establish a general policy by statute. In several measures authorizing specific projects, a government-ownership policy was ordered by special riders. These came to be known as "Long amendments" after their sponsor.

As outlined in Chapter VII, which concerns the Patent Office and other federal agencies, President John F. Kennedy's 1963 statement set a general policy for all agencies except to the extent that they were governed by specific legislation. On the basis of the study made for it by Harbridge House, Inc., the Federal Council for Science and Technology recommended that a new Presidential policy statement, incorporating several changes, be issued but that no legislation be sought. The recommendations were made in November, 1968, before the shift in administrations, and were included in the Council's annual report dated December, 1968, but the report was not distributed until February, 1970. The proposed modifications were minor and would not alter the basic policy concepts. At this writing, no revised Presidential statement has been issued, and there appears to be considerable satisfaction, on the part of industry and the federal agencies involved, with the status quo. As one source commented, "The heat is off."

TOO MUCH MONOPOLY?

Some things that owners do with patents are permissible under the patent laws but not under the antitrust laws. The patentee is entitled to his limited monopoly but must not use it to restrain competition. The dividing line is not always clear.

Richard W. McLaren, assistant attorney general in charge of the Justice Department's Antitrust Division, remarked at a Washington meeting in June, 1969, that it had long been fashionable to say that the patent system was inconsistent with the antitrust laws. "I do not believe that this is necessarily true in all cases," he said. "The basic purposes of both frequently coincide. The patent law seeks to stimulate innovation through reward; the antitrust law seeks to preserve innovation through competition. However, we must recognize that the two systems do, at times, conflict." As examples of practices condemned by the antitrust laws, he mentioned such practices as tying the sale of patented products to the purchase of unpatented material, agreements to refrain from challenging the validity of patents under which no license has been granted, and agreements not to deal in goods that compete with products covered by a patent.

S. Chesterfield Oppenheim, who introduced Mr. McLaren at this meeting—held by the PTC Research Institute of George Washington University—presently heads a study being made by the Institute of patent licensing limitations. Professor Oppenheim was formerly co-chairman of the Attorney General's National Committee to Study the Antitrust Laws, whose massive report, issued in 1955, is a basic source document on patent misuse. Helpful to lawyers is his updated discussion in *Federal Antitrust Laws, Cases and Comments* (West Publishing Company, St. Paul, 1968).

The principal cause of antitrust trouble for patent owners lies in the manner of licensing. Gerald Kadish, a New York lawyer, made a legal survey of patent-antitrust problems, which the Institute published in the Spring 1969 issue of its journal, *IDEA*. Some of his guides and caveats can be briefly summarized as follows.

Patent rights may be transferred by sale of a patent or by the granting of exclusive or nonexclusive licenses to make, use, or sell the invention. The accumulation of any number of patents through one's own research efforts does not violate the antitrust laws. The acquisition of nonexclusive licenses offers little danger, but it is unlawful for a corporation to acquire a patent or an exclusive license from another corporation when the effect may be to lessen competition substantially or tend to create a monopoly.

It is common for patentees to require their licensees to grant back rights under any improvements that the licensees may develop. It would be wise for any company that makes a practice of using grantback clauses to obtain such rights on a nonexclusive basis; it would also be advisable to freely license the rights so acquired to all comers. This would substantially reduce any antitrust liability.

A patentee can decide not to grant licenses. However, any agreement with others to restrict or prohibit the licensing of patents would violate the Sherman Act. There is little, if any, antitrust risk involved in granting licenses restricted to geographical areas.

Field-of-use licenses are sometimes granted, restricting the application of the invention to certain wares, such as the production of milk bottles or fruit jars. Any licensing plan that regulates and suppresses competition among licensees by such restrictions is dangerous.

Limiting a licensee to sell to certain named customers or to a restricted class of purchasers apparently does not violate the antitrust laws. In the absence of some unlawful purpose, such as price-fixing, quantity limitations in licenses are not antitrust violations.

The amount or rate of royalties is within the patentee's discretion, but they are unlawful if they extend beyond a patent's term. Discriminatory rates, requiring higher payments in one area than in another, have been upset when the discrimination was great enough to significantly affect a licensee's ability to compete. It would be a brave or foolhardy patentee who would include a price-fixing provision in a license or include any device that indirectly attempts to control the price at which the licensees may sell.

The tying of the sale of one patented article to the sale of another patented or unpatented article is prohibited. Mandatory "package licensing" is also prohibited. A patentee should never attempt to coerce a licensee into accepting a license that includes more patents than the licensee actually wants. Any attempt by a patentee to prevent a licensee from dealing in products that are competitive with the licensed products violates the antitrust laws.

Once a patentee receives his full reward through the sale of a patented article he loses all control over what the distributor may do with the article. Cross-licensing and patent pools offer advantages, but contracting companies that control a large share of the market are in a vulnerable position. The bringing of infringement suits can be held to be evidence of monopolization if it is found to be part of a scheme to acquire all the important patents in the field and drive out all actual or potential competitors.

Patents, like all things of value, often bring disputes. The arguments involve inventors, corporate owners, lawyers, the courts, the Department of Justice, and occasionally the Patent Office itself. As long as it exists, the patent system is likely to remain a lively field of controversy.

XI

The Patent Wave of the Future

The American patent system is 180 years old and creaks in places but in general is highly regarded by business, industry, and the inventor. The volume of issued patents has been gradually increasing. After numbering began in 1836, the first million patents took about 75 years—to 1911. The second and third millions were reached in about a quarter century each, and it is estimated that the fourth will require only about sixteen years. Patent 3,000,000 was granted in 1961; patent 3,500,000 was issued in March, 1970 (for an echo canceler invented by Bell System engineers as one means of clearing up long-distance conversations); and No. 4,000,000 is expected in 1977 or before.

Among the criticisms of the U.S. patent system are complaints that patents take too long to get and that too many of them are invalidated when questioned in court disputes. To correct this situation, the Patent Office is trying to expedite examination and to raise the quality of issued patents so that they will hold up better in litigation. A third complaint, often voiced by independent inventors, is that patents cost too much, but it seems unlikely that either Patent Office fees or attorneys' charges will be lowered.

Whether or not delays and invalidations can be cured, the Patent Office job promises to keep on growing in several dimensions.

THE PROBLEM OF GROWTH

As technology becomes more complex, the volume of patent applications increases steadily. The figures for fiscal 1960 were 79,331 applications (including applications for designs and plant patents) and 50,607 patents issued. In 1970, for the first time, the number of applications passed 100,000. The total was 100,573, with 66,730 patents issued. At the same time the number of documents that examiners are required to search is increasing geometrically. To keep up with this growing work load, the Patent Office will have to utilize more and more of the electronic technology it guards. There is need for computer help in distinguishing what is new from what has gone before.* There is need for more efficient printing and copying and for better service to, and communication with, the inventor and his lawyer. And there is further growth in a geographical sense, which has resulted in pressures for international arrangements that will make it easier to protect U.S. inventions in other countries as well as in the United States.

Patent Office officials are cautious about making predictions. Projections are difficult because a single revolutionary mechanical advance can greatly modify a forecast made on the basis of current practice. The present has been referred to as a period of turbulence and discontinuity, in which new procedures may alter the picture radically. Nevertheless, a few forecasts are in order.

---

* In June, 1970, the Patent Office granted a contract for the conversion of the texts of 5,000 patents to magnetic computer tape, to be used in research aimed at the computer-aided classification of patents into subject categories. As part of the program, contracts were planned for the taping of an additional 20,000 patents. One object was to investigate the feasibility of using optical character recognition to translate patents from conventional paper to machine-readable form.

1. In recent years the numbers of applications filed and patents issued have increased at the rate of about 3 per cent annually. This trend is expected to continue.
2. Nearly 70 per cent of all recent applications have been "allowed" as patents. Presumably this relationship will continue.
3. With new printing procedures, the forecast is that 80,000 patents will be issued in fiscal 1971.
4. The backlog awaiting or undergoing examination was 187,439 at the end of fiscal 1970. Except for the total of 184,660 at the end of fiscal 1969, this was the lowest since 1953. Efforts to reduce it further and to expedite issuance of the patents already allowed will continue.*
5. In fiscal 1970 the average period between filing and issuance of patents was reduced by one month to twenty-nine months. The hope was that within two years this waiting period could be reduced to twenty-five months and that by 1975 it would be further reduced to eighteen months.

IMPROVEMENTS IN SEARCHING AND PRINTING

At the end of fiscal 1970, the total number of applications in various stages of progress through the Patent Office was 240,667. This figure included 53,228 applications that had been allowed and were awaiting issuance as patents. Some "allowed" accumulation is inevitable because of the clerical work involved and because three months are permitted for payment of the final fee. Also the examiners were approving about a hundred more patents per week in fiscal 1970 than were actually issued. The reason for this was that in calendar 1969 and fiscal 1970 the weekly output of patents was held to 1,300, partly by limitations in the budget and partly by the

---

* In trying to reduce its backlog of patents awaiting examination or undergoing examination, the Patent Office has achieved more "disposals" than current filing totals. By disposal is meant approval of an application for issuance as a patent, or its final rejection and relegation to "abandoned" status. In fiscal 1970 the number of disposals reached 103,692.

capacity of the Government Printing Office. It was expected that the printing backlog would be cleared up in calendar 1971.

Changes inaugurated with little fanfare in August, 1970, seemed to forecast not only a much greater patent output but mechanization of searching. There was even a new look for the patent itself. On a limited scale, computer photocomposition of patents was started. At the same time, the Patent Office used the computer tape to begin building up a "data base," or library of technical information comprising the full texts of the allowed patent applications.

When the shift began, William E. Schuyler, Jr., Commissioner of Patents, commented: "This means that by 1975 the Patent Office will have a full-text data base of more than one quarter of a million patents in machine-readable form which may be used in computerized classification and search systems."

Step by step, the new procedure for computerized printing was as follows: After approving an application, the Patent Office sent it to a contractor in Fort Washington, Pennsylvania. Workers in Fort Washington typed the application text on magnetic tape, with typographical instructions to the computer, and sent the tape to the Government Printing Office in Washington. The Government Printing Office ran the magnetic tape through a computer under control of a master typography program and through the Linotron, a machine developed for the agency by the Mergenthaler Linotype Company and C.B.S. Laboratories. The Linotron generated photocomposed pages, producing a camera copy of the text. The camera copy was sent to another contractor in Silver Spring, Maryland, who made offset plates from the camera copy, reproduced the drawings by the offset process, printed and bound the patents, and delivered them to the Patent Office. Meantime the magnetic tape went from the Printing Office to the Patent Office for use as the data base. The new process began on a small scale, and the Government Printing Office continued temporarily to turn out the texts of most patents by the usual "hot metal" and letterpress methods. The Silver Spring contractor added the drawings to these patents and did the binding.

Introduction of computerized printing was accompanied by a "face-lifting"—adoption of a new patent format, with a front page summarizing essentials of the invention. Until then, the familiar patent had consisted of sheets of drawings (if there were drawings), followed by printed pages containing the abstract, detailed description, and claims. The first sheet included the patent number and date, the names and addresses of the inventor and any assignee, one drawing (if there were drawings), and the abstract. Other data on the first page included the classification numbers, field of search, references cited, and names of the examiners and attorneys. On the following sheets all the drawing figures, the disclosure, and the claims appeared.

In the change-over period, the weekly patent output was held below 1,300, but the hope was that it could be raised to 1,750.

The mechanization of the search process will be an important aid in reducing the backlog and decreasing the time period between application and filing, but, even if the necessary data can be retrieved by machine from documents and electronic memories, the human mind must make the decisions, and the chief reliance will still be on a staff of skilled examiners. In recent years the fast-growing number of documents to be checked has greatly increased the examiners' burden. The number of U.S. patents in the search files, including those needed for cross-references, is nearly 10 million, and a projection shows a total of nearly 12.5 million by 1980. The total of U.S. and foreign patents, now about 17.5 million, can be projected in various ways, depending on whether counterparts are eliminated when the same invention is patented in various countries, and on the degree of cross-referencing. The forecasts for 1980 range from about 22.5 million to almost 45 million. In addition, the nonpatent foreign and domestic technical literature in the classified files now approximates 350,000 documents and is sure to mount.

The output per examiner under all this burden is necessarily slowed. In 1962 it was calculated that in the preceding thirty years the average annual number of disposals per assistant examiner—the man doing the detailed work—had been cut in half. About 81 per cent of an examiner's working day is now spent on the examining task. It has been calculated that each disposal (issuance or abandonment) takes eighteen hours of an assistant examiner's time, including that of his supervisor. The time per case varies with changes in procedure but has remained almost constant for three years. The greatest promise for speeding up the examining process therefore lies in computerized searching with the data base procedure described above. Some progress in mechanization has already been made, as outlined in Chapter III. If an examiner can explore all the prior art by pressing a few buttons, much of his time will be saved. The question of whether the computers are to be installed in the Patent Office or miles away will be determined by a study of their cost-effectiveness. Proximity is not important.

The average number of examiners was 1,170 early in 1970. To continue reducing the backlog, from twenty to thirty more examiners must be added to the staff each year. If an effort is made at more rapid reduction, even more examiners will be required. The examiner turnover has been lessening recently with improved government salaries and a Patent Office policy of early advancement to full signatory authority, which gives a feeling of independence to examiners. Many, however, still resign to enter patent practice.

IMPROVEMENTS IN SERVICES

The major improvements in services planned by the Patent Office are based on the use of punched cards, microfiche, and the "aperture" cards described in Chapter III. Eventually industry will be supplied with classified decks of punched cards, each containing eight apertures in which microfilmed copies of the text and drawings of a single patent are inserted. One card has enough capacity to display an entire patent of average size, which can then be read with the aid of a desk viewer. A subscription service will provide the cards by class and subclass. In addition to convenience in storage, handling, and retrieval, the aperture card should cost much less than a full-sized paper copy of a patent.

It is possible that the use of aperture cards will make possible the establishment of search centers in major industrial areas. These local search centers will not only enable the public to do its searching with aperture cards rather than full-sized paper copies of U.S. patents but will utilize microfilmed copies of foreign patents, which represents an impressive saving in space over the bound and unbound copies that must be stored in vertical files.

The expectation is that the future will bring more demand for filmed copies of documents required in searching than for paper. The Patent Office has already begun recording incoming applications on microfiche—in which there is space for sixty-four images on a single card—and the system can also be used to reproduce applications for foreign filings.

PROPOSED LAWS AND TREATIES

Proposed treaties affecting future international operations of the Patent Office have been discussed in Chapter V. The so-called patent reform act, now pending in a tempered version, is treated in Chapter X. The recommendations of the

President's Commission on the patent system are outlined in Appendix C. Among the proposals not incorporated in bills now pending in committee, but likely to be raised in the future, are

1. The protection of designs and software by means other than patents
2. An optional deferred examination system
3. Modified court review procedure
4. Appointment of civil commissioners and an advisory council.

After a detailed study had been made of the 1966 report of the President's Commission on the Patent System by the PTC Research Institute of George Washington University, the Institute's director, Dr. L. James Harris, proposed a dual patent system and a Validity Court. The major objectives of the proposed dual patent program* are

1. To encourage inventions, investment in their development, and their commercial utilization;
2. To provide the independent inventor, or the small businessman, and the larger company an opportunity to choose patent protection more suitable to their peculiar needs by offering two types of patent: a "long-term" and a "short-term" patent;
3. To make the patent a much more dependable property by introducing the concept of "incontestability";
4. To simplify the method of challenging a patent after issue, and reduce the sometimes diverse results of multiple court contests, by establishing a Court of Validity to act on questions of validity;
5. To place greater reliance on the Patent Office product by grounding the concept of "incontestability" in a high quality of Patent Office examination.

A short-lived, reliable patent would, it is believed, serve the best interests of both the new small businessman and the inde-

* As published in *IDEA* for Spring 1969 and in the 1969 conference issue.

pendent inventor, both interested in the short-lived market and the uncomplicated invention not requiring a long period for development.

The proposal includes a long-term, 17-year patent, incontestable five years after issue, and a short-term, 7-year patent incontestable one year after issue. In the respective 5-year and 1-year periods, the patents would be subject to current practice but would have their validity tried only before the proposed Validity Court. Thereafter they would be incontestable unless successfully challenged before the Validity Court on grounds of (a) prior invention or (b) fraud or deception. Dr. Harris believes his dual patent program would reduce the costs, duration, and uncertainties of patent litigation.

A White House Task Force on Antitrust Policy, appointed by President Lyndon B. Johnson, submitted a report in 1968 recommending legislation that, among other things, would require a patent holder to license all applicants at nondiscriminatory rates if it licenses anyone. The report, signed by Phil C. Neal, dean of the University of Chicago Law School, as chairman of the task force, was made public by the Justice Department in May, 1969, without comment. Among the recommendations is compulsory filing of all patent licenses with the Commissioner of Patents.

INVENTING IN THE 1970's

What will inventions of the future be like? Outstanding examples among those of the last twenty-five years are the transistor, the laser, integrated circuitry, and two commercial successes: xerography and the Polaroid Land camera.

A hint as to the direction future inventions will take has been given by recent patents on the approach to artificial intelligence through electronic simulation of the functions of the neuron, or human nerve cell. For example, circuits invented by engineers to simulate human learning, forgetting, and decision-making are intended to serve in an automatic monitoring and early warning system, with varied uses in industry and space. A patented electronic machine developed in Great Britain is intended to explore and react with its environment, using a figurative eye that might consist of photocells. Suggested applications are control of a chemical plant, regulation of traffic, and a reading system. The inventors hope that, when the machine is subjected to figurative rewards, inhibitions, and punishments, it will learn to exercise foresight.

Members of the National Inventors Council, a body of private citizens who advise the Secretary of Commerce on matters relating to inventions and patents, were polled informally in 1968 on the subject of notable recent inventions.* They cited, among others, the basic oxygen steel-making process, holography (lensless photography), and fiber optics. Space and atomic developments were also mentioned. When members of the council were queried the following year on the future course of invention, they said that inventors in the next decade should be motivated by the needs of society rather than by the lure of technological advance for its own sake. Suggested fields for future investigation included crime prevention, the control of pollution, satisfying the world's hunger with synthetic foods, stabilizing population, solutions to drug and alcoholic addiction, the needs of developing nations, and vastly improved communication. Dr. Charles Stark Draper, the council's chairman, remarked that inventors could have a great influence on human history by providing means for man to make significant changes in his species.

Daniel V. De Simone, the National Inventors Council's executive director, listed some biotechnological inventions (concerning the relationships between humans and machines)

---

* Parts of the summary of the National Inventors Council's thoughts on the future course of invention are copyright 1969 by the New York Times Company and are reprinted with permission.

but pointed to the dangers in their indiscriminate use. Among such inventions were: genetic engineering to control hereditary defects and to create the kind of population *someone* wants; fertility control through sexual manipulation (fewer females); primitive artificial life; nonnarcotic, personality-changing drugs; artificial replacement organs for the human body; biochemicals to stimulate growth of new organs and limbs; drugs to increase (or decrease) intelligence; creation of intelligent animals for low-grade labor; direct communication between brain and computer; education (voluntary or involuntary) by direct recording on the brain.

Other possibilities envisioned by members of the National Inventors Council:

- Circuits (referred to as "cellistors") creating computers and communication systems from living cells
- The almost complete elimination of money through use of nontransferable identity cards to be inserted in reading machines connected to a central computer
- Bioelectric means similar to that in electric eels to power cardiac pacemakers
- Supersonic, radar-controlled, radar-guided transmission of matter, both inanimate (including automobiles) and animate (including humans) from a starting point to a specified destination
- Economical liquefying of coal at the mine source
- Attention-discriminators that would enable people to concentrate only on subjects of importance to them
- A plasma arc roadbuilder, with which a stream of highly ionized gas would remove all vegetation from the roadbed and fuse the ground to support a load
- A robot vacuum cleaner that could be let loose in a room full of furniture

In a report, *Invention and the Patent System,* published in 1964 by the Joint Economic Committee of Congress, Dr. S. C. Gilfillan listed many inventions not yet made and others requiring improvement. These included: electroluminescence and chemical luminescence for the production of light at a reduced cost in heat and energy; shallow geophysical prospecting for the recovery of lost nonmetallic objects; microprinting for the production of little books; and voice-operated writing machines.

PATENT COMMISSIONER'S DREAM

On February 19, 1963, an imaginative Commissioner of Patents, David L. Ladd, looked deep into the future, and shared his vision with the Delaware Council of Engineering Societies at a meeting in Wilmington, Delaware. His vision began with a fanciful visit to a new Patent Office building. To some extent this part of the dream has already been realized in the form of the Crystal Plaza quarters now occupied by the Patent Office in Arlington County, Virginia. When the speaker proceeded with his mental trip through the offices, however, he presented a picture of automation and examination by computer that was still years ahead as this book went to press. In conducting his listeners on this fictitious tour, Mr. Ladd said in part:

We move then to another section of the building, where there is a large number of computers and other formidable looking equipment. The Assistant Commissioner for Research meets us to show us around. First, he explains to us that all American and the overwhelming majority of foreign patents, and most of the important technological publications are received in the Patent Office. They are microfilmed with the use of ultra micro reduction techniques and stored in a graphic image retrieval machine. Those in foreign languages are translated by machine and the translation is stored in microcopy with the originals. As a second step, the documents are scanned and analyzed by machine and the information stored in huge memories.

Patent searches are conducted with these files. In fact, these patent searches are conducted in a startling way. The application itself has been automatically scanned, and the search questions are formulated by machines and answered by machines. When the selected relevant references have been identified and listed, another computer system matches the subject matter of the application and the references against the technical qualifications of the various examiners, and the case is then routed to the examiner most qualified to handle the technical questions involved in that particular case. In very complex patent applications, crossing several technological fields, the application is routed to several examiners who pool their knowledges and expertise in examining that one application.

We then move over into the examiners' wing. The examiners themselves each have individual rooms; but they have rather special equipment. First, each room has a television screen. From a simple switchboard on his desk, the examiner can call for the display on a screen of any document in the microfilm files which we saw earlier. Moreover, he can, if he wishes, ask that any given collection of documents on a single technical subject be displayed serially on his screen, or indeed, in the order of probable usefulness to the examiner's search. As he sees an additional document which he believes to have relevance to the application which he is examining, he may then turn to a print-out device which is a part of his control console and have instantly a hard copy for his use; or, of course, he may have a hard copy of any of the references which the machine-assisted search has identified.

At this point, we musingly remember the days when the examiner spent a substantial portion of his time riffling through stacks and stacks of paper by hand. For example, in 1963, there were 300 main classes in the Patent Office classification system, 62,000 subclasses, over 3,000,000 American patents each cross-referenced into several subclasses, more than 4,000,000 foreign patents and a lot of open nonpatent literature —in all, over 65,000,000 pages. (In those days the Patent Office had to have an additional 3,000 square feet of space annually to house all that paper.)

We discover, too, that this magnificent information retrieval system is not confined to the use of the Patent Office alone. We learn that private companies and research groups and universities throughout the country have the same kind of television hook-up to the microfilm files and to the computers as the examiners have. From anywhere in the United States, a full picture of the state of the art in any field can be obtained from these files in the Patent Office. In fact, many companies have placed standing orders for any documents in the areas of technology in which they are interested, and these documents are reproduced instantaneously by print-out apparatus in their own labs and offices as soon as they are programmed into the system.

And what has happened to our cumbersome method of exchanging documents with other countries? This system in the United States Patent Office has been integrated with similar documentation centers abroad. The reference documents themselves move between the U.S. Patent Office, foreign patent offices, and foreign documentation centers in machine language form. The United States has entered into agreements with some foreign countries that each country will be responsible for disseminating the technological documents originating in each country to the patent offices and documentation centers of other countries on an exchange basis. Optical scanning at the originating office provides the machine language medium to serve as in-put to automatic translation machines so that signals coming from Germany, say,—by satellite, of course—arrive at the United States Patent Office in English; and signals from the United States arrive at the German Patent Office in German.

Valuable and specialized document collections in libraries, museums, universities, and research institutes can be searched and studied in this manner; distances and foreign languages present no problems. Actual equipment in museums can also be viewed and photographic details instantaneously recorded for the examiner's later study and reference.

Walking on down to another section of the examiner's wing, we find that the method of examining and adjudicating patent applications has changed drastically since the old days back in the 1960's. We walk into a room where an examiner again sits before a screen with a case laid out before him, together with all the references. We discover that he is discussing the case with a patent lawyer in San Francisco. The patent lawyer himself, in his studio room in San Francisco, has a similar screen and microphone set-up so that the examiner and the lawyer have two-way visual and audio communication. The two men are discussing the case—the lawyer explaining the disclosure and arguing for a broader scope to the claims; the examiner is pointing out the similarities of the prior art references and contending that the claims should not be granted (allowed) in so broad a form. As we stand there, the two men reach an understanding and agree that a final amendment shall be filed by the attorney and the case, as agreed upon, allowed. As the examiner gathers his papers to leave the desk, we notice that he has made no elaborate notes and he explains to us that the entire communication has been transcribed and the transcription forms a part of the formal record in the case. That transcription will be automatically coded and filed, easily retrievable to assemble a complete history of the prosecution if such a need arises.

Gone are the days when lawyers filed elaborate memoranda in support of their amendments and the examiner returned long written formal actions, and the result was a long delay between the time the application was filed and the patent issued. And a good thing it is too; for technology is moving now even faster than it was in the 1960's. People need decisions faster now on their patent applications just as they need quick dissemination of information about the latest advances in all the useful arts.

Because of this service, the administration of research and development has been revolutionized. Most companies will not authorize a research and development project until a search has been made. Much expensive work is thereby avoided and the companies get more for their research and development dollar. The great avalanche of technical literature has been harnessed, its energy used not to oppress, but to free the technician, engineer and scientist. Patents issue promptly after the applications are filed, and investment and research decisions are quickly reached. The Patent Office has become a throbbing, pulsing center of the thrust of technological change.

What has happened to the examiner, scientist, inventor and design engineer whose perception has extended world wide, whose library includes most of the relevant documents in all languages, whose access to information is prompt and exhaustive? He is now more important than ever, for his professional practice now encompasses a greater range of information on his technical specialty than ever before. His technical judgment is more valuable; his education more thorough and his status and recognition—appropriately—beyond that of his intellectual forebears.

Intoxicated? I hope so. Skeptical? You should be! Hopeful? We must be! For the Patent Office, which since its inception has fostered the useful arts, must now provide not only the incentives but the resources and services for the technological growth and, yes, the technological competition upon which our prosperity and security certainly depend.

Mr. Ladd's glowing projection of the future Patent Office will in time no doubt be realized in its essentials, if not in all its detail. Certainly the agency's mounting task demands the best equipment that technology can produce—the computer, the video screen, the Picturephone, and (overhead) the satellite. More important, it demands a skilled staff of technicians, examiners, and administrators—and sympathy and money from Congress. With all these blessings, the Patent Office should continue to supply what American society expects: protection for the inventor—without too much monopoly—and the stimulation of technological progress.

Appendix A

Patent Office Career Opportunities

Career jobs in the Patent Office are all filled through Civil Service Commission procedures. Inquiry as to openings and qualifications may be addressed to the Personnel Officer, U.S. Patent Office, Washington, D.C., 20231.

For patent examiner positions, the entering grades for recent college graduates are Civil Service GS-5 and GS-7, depending on scholastic standing. Starting salaries are about $8,000 in GS-5, which requires four years of college engineering, chemistry, or physics. The entering salary in GS-7, which has higher requirements, is about $10,000. These are career jobs promising regular promotions for satisfactory work, and it is possible for an examiner to progress to GS-15, with a top salary of about $29,000.

The duties of an examiner are as follows. He reads the disclosures in an application and examines the drawings, if there are any. He studies the "claims" (definitions of the invention) at the end of the application, searches the "prior art" (chiefly earlier patents and publications) to see whether the claimed invention is new, and applies legal principles and court decisions to determine whether the claimed invention is useful and whether it involves patentable invention. If the application passes the three tests of patentability—novelty, utility, and invention—he recommends that a patent be allowed. Or the examiner rejects those claims that do not meet the three tests. The procedure is covered in detail in the *Manual of Patent Examining Procedure,* available on an annual subscription basis from the Superintendent of Documents, U.S. Government Printing Office.

To recruit examiners, the Patent Office sends representatives to many college campuses to interview prospective applicants. In some years as many as two hundred colleges awarding engineering degrees have been visited, but the lowered turnover rate has reduced the number currently to about fifty. The recruiters include Personnel Division employees but are chiefly examiners. They are prepared to supply students information on openings in other Commerce Department agencies, and representatives of those agencies reciprocate by informing applicants about Patent Office jobs.

New examiners go through a two-week training program, six months of on-the-job training, and both basic and advanced Patent Office Academy programs. In recent years between 150 and 200 new examiners have been hired annually. While the turnover has dropped, it has been relatively high because many examiners get degrees in night law school and resign from the government to join patent law firms or the patent departments of corporations. The Patent Office pays about three-quarters of the cost of night law-school courses, but this amount must be refunded by any examiner who leaves the Patent Office within five years.

Examinations for most scientific and technical positions do not include written tests. The Civil Service Commission issues announcements that describe the type of work, and qualifications for different positions, as well as instructions as to filing applications. Other competitive jobs in the Patent Office are filled from eligibles on registers of the Civil Service Commission, compiled after entrance examinations, most of which are written.

The Patent Office grants step increases in pay to several hundred professional and clerical employees each year and makes, in addition, cash awards of $200 or over for special performance. The Personnel Division conducts a number of staff development programs to enable both professional and clerical employees to take on more responsibility and advance their civil service ratings.

Appendix B

Extracts from the Patent Law

Article I, Section 8, of the Constitution provides that "The Congress shall have Power . . . To promote the Progress of Science and useful Arts, by securing for limited Times to Authors and Inventors the exclusive Right to their respective Writings and Discoveries."

The principal patent law adopted under this authority and now in force is *United States Code: Title 35—Patents.* A number of other statutes, including several relating to the courts, the Atomic Energy Commission, and the National Aeronautics and Space Administration, regulate specific matters concerning patents.

The booklet *Patent Laws,* available from the Superintendent of Documents, U.S. Government Printing Office, contains the full text of Title 35 and references to other statutes. Limitations of space do not permit reprinting the complete law here. However, pertinent sections of interest to prospective employees of the Patent Office, to inventors, and to prospective inventors are reproduced below. These pertain to: establishment, officers, and functions of the Patent Office; patent fees; patentability of inventions; application for patent; examination of application; issue of patent; plant patents; and designs (from Chapters 1, 4, 10, 11, 12, 14, 15, and 16 of Title 35). Chapters not included here are concerned with such matters as inventions made in foreign countries, procedure and practice before the Patent Office, joint inventors, court review, infringement, remedies and damages, the secrecy of inventions affecting national security, applications filed, and reissued patents.

ESTABLISHMENT, OFFICERS, FUNCTIONS

§ 1. *Establishment*

The Patent Office shall continue as an office in the Department of Commerce, where records, books, drawings, specifications, and other papers and things pertaining to patents and to trade-mark registrations shall be kept and preserved, except as otherwise provided by law. . . .

§ 3. *Officers and employees*

A Commissioner of Patents, one first assistant commissioner, two assistant commissioners, and not more than fifteen examiners-in-chief, shall be appointed by the President, by and with the advice and consent of the Senate. The assistant commissioners shall perform the duties pertaining to the office of commissioner assigned to them by the Commissioner. The first assistant commissioner, or, in the event of a vacancy in that office, the assistant commissioner senior in date of appointment, shall fill the office of Commissioner during a vacancy in that office until a Commissioner is appointed and takes office. The Secretary of Commerce, upon the nomination of the Commissioner in accordance with law, shall appoint all other officers and employees.

The Secretary of Commerce may vest in himself the functions of the Patent Office and its officers and employees specified in this title and may from time to time authorize their performance by any other officer or employee. The Secretary of Commerce is authorized to fix the per annum rate of basic compensation of each examiner-in-chief in the Patent Office at not in excess of the maximum scheduled rate provided for positions in grade 17 of the General Schedule of the Classification Act of 1949, as amended.

§ 4. *Restrictions on officers and employees as to interest in patents*

Officers and employees of the Patent Office shall be incapable, during the period of their appointments and for one year thereafter, of applying for a patent and of acquiring, directly or indirectly, except by inheritance or bequest, any patent or any right or interest in any patent, issued or to be issued by the Office. In patents applied thereafter they shall not be entitled to any priority date earlier than one year after the termination of their appointment. . . .

§ 6. *Duties of Commissioner*

The Commissioner, under the direction of the Secretary of Commerce, shall superintend or perform all duties required by law respecting the granting and issuing of patents and the registration of trade-marks; and he shall have charge of property belonging to the Patent Office. He may, subject to the approval of the Secretary of Commerce, establish regulations, not inconsistent with law, for the conduct of proceedings in the Patent Office.

§ 7. *Board of Appeals*

The examiners-in-chief shall be persons of competent legal knowledge and scientific ability. The Commissioner, the assistant commissioners, and the examiners-in-chief shall constitute a Board of Appeals, which, on written appeal of the applicant, shall review adverse decisions of examiners upon applications for patents. Each appeal shall be heard by at least three members of the Board of Appeals, the members hearing such appeal to be designated by the Commissioner. The Board of Appeals has sole power to grant rehearings.

Whenever the Commissioner considers it necessary to maintain the work of the Board of Appeals current, he may designate any patent examiner of the primary grade or higher, having the requisite ability, to serve as examiner-in-chief for periods not exceeding six months each. An examiner so designated shall be qualified to act as a member of the Board of Appeals. Not more than one such primary examiner shall be a member of the Board of Appeals hearing an appeal. The Secretary of Commerce is authorized to fix the per annum rate of basic compensation of each designated examiner-in-chief in the Patent Office at not in excess of the maximum scheduled rate provided for positions in grade 16 of the General Schedule of the Classification Act of 1949, as amended. The per annum rate of basic compensation of each designated examiner-in-chief shall be adjusted, at the close of the period for which he was designated to act as examiner-in-chief, to the per annum rate of basic compensation which he would have been receiving at the close of such period if such designation had not been made. . . .

PATENT FEES

§ 41. *Patent fees*

(a) The Commissioner shall charge the following fees:

1. On filing each application for an original patent, except in design cases, $65; in addition, on filing or on presentation at any other time, $10 for each claim in independent form which is in excess of one, and $2 for each claim (whether independent or dependent) which is in excess of ten. Errors in payment of the additional fees may be rectified in accordance with regulations of the Commissioner.

2. For issuing each original or reissue patent, except in design cases, $100; in addition, $10 for each page (or portion thereof) of specification as printed, and $2 for each sheet of drawing.

3. In design cases:

   a. On filing each design application, $20.

   b. On issuing each design patent: For three years and six months, $10; for seven years, $20; and for fourteen years, $30.

4. On filing each application for the reissue of a patent, $65; in addition, on filing or on presentation at any other time, $10 for each claim in independent form which is in excess of the number of independent claims of the original patent, and $2 for each claim (whether independent or dependent) which is in excess of ten and also in excess of the number of claims of the original patent. Errors in payment of the additional fees may be rectified in accordance with regulations of the Commissioner.

5. On filing each disclaimer, $15.

6. On appeal for the first time from the examiner to the Board of Appeals, $50; in addition, on filing a brief in support of the appeal, $50.

7. On filing each petition for the revival of an abandoned application for a patent or for the delayed payment of the fee for issuing each patent, $15.

8. For certificate under section 255 or under section 256 of this title, $15.

9. As available and if in print: For uncertified printed copies of specifications and drawings of patents (except design patents), 50 cents per copy; for design patents, 20 cents per copy; the Commissioner may establish a charge not to exceed $1 per copy for patents in excess of twenty-five pages of drawings and specifications and for plant patents printed in color; special rates for libraries specified in section 13 of this title, $50 for patents issued in one year. The Commissioner may, without charge, provide applicants with copies of specifications and drawings of patents when referred to in a notice under section 132.

10. For recording every assignment, agreement, or other paper relating to the property in a patent or application, $20; where the document relates to more than one patent or application, $3 for each additional item.

11. For each certificate, $1.

(b) The Commissioner may establish charges for copies of records, publications, or services furnished by the Patent Office, not specified above.

(c) The fees prescribed by or under this section shall apply to any other Government department or agency, or officer thereof, except that the Commissioner may waive the payment of any fee for services or materials in cases of occasional or incidental requests by a Government department or agency, or officer thereof. . . .

PATENTABILITY OF INVENTIONS

§ 100. *Definitions*

When used in this title unless the context otherwise indicates—

(a) The term "invention" means invention or discovery.

(b) The term "process" means process, art or method, and includes a new use of a known process, machine, manufacture, composition of matter, or material.

(c) The terms "United States" and "this country" mean the United States of America, its territories and possessions.

(d) The word "patentee" includes not only the patentee to

whom the patent was issued but also the successors in title to the patentee.

§ 101. *Inventions patentable*

Whoever invents or discovers any new and useful process, machine, manufacture, or composition of matter, or any new and useful improvement thereof, may obtain a patent therefor, subject to the conditions and requirements of this title.

§ 102. *Conditions for patentability; novelty and loss of right to patent*

A person shall be entitled to a patent unless—

(a) the invention was known or used by others in this country, or patented or described in a printed publication in this or a foreign country, before the invention thereof by the applicant for patent, or

(b) the invention was patented or described in a printed publication in this or a foreign country or in public use or on sale in this country, more than one year prior to the date of the application for patent in the United States, or

(c) he has abandoned the invention, or

(d) the invention was first patented or caused to be patented by the applicant or his legal representatives or assigns in a foreign country prior to the date of the application for patent in this country on an application filed more than twelve months before the filing of the application in the United States, or

(e) the invention was described in a patent granted on an application for patent by another filed in the United States before the invention thereof by the applicant for patent, or

(f) he did not himself invent the subject matter sought to be patented, or

(g) before the applicant's invention thereof the invention was made in this country by another who had not abandoned, suppressed, or concealed it. In determining priority of invention there shall be considered not only the respective dates of conception and reduction to practice of the invention, but also the reasonable diligence of one who was first to conceive and last to reduce to practice, from a time prior to conception by the other.

§ 103. *Conditions for patentability; non-obvious subject matter*
A patent may not be obtained though the invention is not identically disclosed or described as set forth in section 102 of this title, if the differences between the subject matter sought to be patented and the prior art are such that the subject matter as a whole would have been obvious at the time the invention was made to a person having ordinary skill in the art to which said subject matter pertains. Patentability shall not be negatived by the manner in which the invention was made. . . .

APPLICATION FOR PATENT

§ 111. *Application for patent*
Application for patent shall be made by the inventor, except as otherwise provided in this title, in writing to the Commissioner. Such application shall include: (1) a specification as prescribed by section 112 of this title: (2) a drawing as prescribed by section 113 of this title; and (3) an oath by the applicant as prescribed by section 115 of this title. The application must be signed by the applicant and accompanied by the fee required by law.

§ 112. *Specification*
The specification shall contain a written description of the invention, and of the manner and process of making and using it, in such full, clear, concise, and exact terms as to enable any person skilled in the art to which it pertains, or with which it is most nearly connected, to make and use the same, and shall set forth the best mode contemplated by the inventor of carrying out his invention.

The specification shall conclude with one or more claims particularly pointing out and distinctly claiming the subject matter which the applicant regards as his invention. A claim may be written in independent or dependent form, and if in dependent form, it shall be construed to include all the limitations of the claim incorporated by reference into the dependent claim.

An element in a claim for a combination may be expressed as a means or step for performing a specified function without the recital of structure, material, or acts in support thereof, and such claim shal be construed to cover the corresponding structure, material, or acts described in the specification and equivalents thereof.

§ 113. *Drawings*
When the nature of the case admits, the applicant shall furnish a drawing.

§ 114. *Models, specimens*
The Commissioner may require the applicant to furnish a model of convenient size to exhibit advantageously the several parts of his invention.

When the invention relates to a composition of matter, the Commissioner may require the applicant to furnish specimens or ingredients for the purpose of inspection or experiment.

§ 115. *Oath of applicant*
The applicant shall make oath that he believes himself to be the original and first inventor of the process, machine, manufacture, or composition of matter, or improvement thereof, for which he solicits a patent; and shall state of what country he is a citizen. Such oath may be made before any person in the United States authorized by law to administer oaths, or, when made in a foreign country, before any diplomatic or consular officer of the United States authorized to administer oaths, or before any officer having an official seal and authorized to administer oaths in the foreign country in which the applicant may be, whose authority shall be proved by certificate of a diplomatic or consular officer of the United States, and such oath shall be valid if it complies with the laws of the state or country where made. When the application is made as provided in this title by a person other than the inventor, the oath may be so varied in form that it can be made by him. . . .

§ 122. *Confidential status of applications*
Applications for patents shall be kept in confidence by the Patent Office and no information concerning the same given without authority of the applicant or owner unless necessary to carry out the provisions of any Act of Congress or in such special circumstances as may be determined by the Commissioner. . . .

EXAMINATION OF APPLICATION

§ 131. *Examination of application*

The Commissioner shall cause an examination to be made of the application and the alleged new invention; and if on such examination it appears that the applicant is entitled to a patent under the law, the Commissioner shall issue a patent therefor.

§ 132. *Notice of rejection; reexamination*

Whenever, on examination, any claim for a patent is rejected, or any objection or requirement made, the Commissioner shall notify the applicant thereof, stating the reasons for such rejection, or objection or requirement, together with such information and references as may be useful in judging of the propriety of continuing the prosecution of his application; and if after receiving such notice, the applicant persists in his claim for a patent, with or without amendment, the application shall be reexamined. No amendment shall introduce new matter into the disclosure of the invention.

§ 133. *Time for prosecuting application*

Upon failure of the applicant to prosecute the application within six months after any action therein, of which notice has been given or mailed to the applicant, or within such shorter time, not less than thirty days, as fixed by the Commissioner in such action, the application shall be regarded as abandoned by the parties thereto, unless it be shown to the satisfaction of the Commissioner that such delay was unavoidable.

§ 134. *Appeal to the Board of Appeals*

An applicant for a patent, any of whose claims has been twice rejected, may appeal from the decision of the primary examiner to the Board of Appeals, having once paid the fee for such appeal.

§ 135. *Interferences*

(a) Whenever an application is made for a patent which, in the opinion of the Commissioner, would interfere with any pending application, or with any unexpired patent, he shall give notice thereof to the applicants, or applicant and patentee, as the case may be. The question of priority of invention shall be determined by a board of patent interferences (consisting of three examiners of interferences) whose decision, if adverse to the claim of an applicant, shall constitute the final refusal by the Patent Office of the claims involved, and the Commissioner may issue a patent to the applicant who is adjudged the prior inventor. A final judgment adverse to a patentee from which no appeal or other review has been or can be taken or had shall constitute cancellation of the claims involved from the patent, and notice thereof shall be endorsed on copies of the patent thereafter distributed by the Patent Office.

(b) A claim which is the same as, or for the same or substantially the same subject matter as, a claim of an issued patent may not be made in any application unless such a claim is made prior to one year from the date on which the patent was granted.

(c) Any agreement or understanding between parties to an interference, including any collateral agreements referred to therein, made in connection with or in contemplation of the termination of the interference, shall be in writing and a true copy thereof filed in the Patent Office before the termination of the interference as between the said parties to the agreement or understanding. If any party filing the same so requests, the copy shall be kept separate from the file of the interference, and made available only to Government agencies on written request, or to any person on a showing of good cause. Failure to file the copy of such agreement or understanding shall render permanently unenforceable such agreement or understanding and any patent of such parties involved in the interference or any patent subsequently issued on any application of such parties so involved. The Commissioner may, however, on a showing of good cause for failure to file within the time prescribed, permit the filing of the agreement or understanding during the six-month period subsequent to the termination of the interference as between the parties to the agreement or understanding.

The Commissioner shall give notice to the parties or their attorneys of record, a reasonable time prior to said termination, of the filing requirement of this section. If the Commissioner gives such notice at a later time, irrespective of the right to file such agreement or understanding within the six-month period on a showing of good cause, the parties may file such agreement or understanding within sixty days of the receipt of such notice.

Any discretionary action of the Commissioner under this subsection shall be reviewable under section 10 of the Administrative Procedure Act. . . .

ISSUE OF PATENT

§ 151. *Issue of patent*

If it appears that applicant is entitled to a patent under the law, a written notice of allowance of the application shall be given or mailed to the applicant. The notice shall specify a sum, constituting the issue fee or a portion thereof, which shall be paid within three months thereafter.

Upon payment of this sum the patent shall issue, but if payment is not timely made, the application shall be regarded as abandoned.

Any remaining balance of the issue fee shall be paid within three months from the sending of a notice thereof and, if not paid, the patent shall lapse at the termination of this three-month period. In calculating the amount of a remaining balance, charges for a page or less may be disregarded.

If any payment required by this section is not timely made, but is submitted with the fee for delayed payment within three months after the due date and sufficient cause is shown for the late payment, it may be accepted by the Commissioner as though no abandonment or lapse had ever occurred.

§ 152. *Issue of patent to assignee*

Patents may be granted to the assignee of the inventor of record in the Patent Office, upon the application made and the specification sworn to by the inventor, except as otherwise provided in this title. . . .

§ 154. *Contents and term of patent*

Every patent shall contain a short title of the invention and a grant to the patentee, his heirs or assigns, for the term of seventeen years, subject to the payment of issue fees as provided for in this title, of the right to exclude others from making, using, or selling the invention throughout the United States, referring to the specifications for the particulars thereof. A copy of the specifications and drawings shall be annexed to the patent and be a part thereof. . . .

PLANT PATENTS

§ 161. *Patents for plants*

Whoever invents or discovers and asexually reproduces any distinct and new variety of plant, including cultivated sports, mutants, hybrids, and newly found seedlings, other than a tuber propagated plant or a plant found in an uncultivated state, may obtain a patent therefor, subject to the conditions and requirements of this title.

The provisions of this title relating to patents for inventions shall apply to patents for plants, except as otherwise provided.

§ 162. *Description, claim*

No plant patent shall be declared invalid for noncompliance with section 112 of this title if the description is as complete as is reasonably possible.

The claim in the specification shall be in formal terms to the plant shown and described.

§ 163. *Grant*

In the case of a plant patent the grant shall be of the right to exclude others from asexually reproducing the plant or selling or using the plant so reproduced.

§ 164. *Assistance of Department of Agriculture*

The President may by Executive order direct the Secretary of Agriculture, in accordance with the requests of the Commissioner, for the purpose of carrying into effect the provisions of this title with respect to plants (1) to furnish available information of the Department of Agriculture, (2) to conduct through the appropriate bureau or division of the Department research upon special problems, or (3) to detail to the Commissioner officers and employees of the Department. . . .

DESIGNS

§ 171. *Patents for designs*

Whoever invents any new, original and ornamental design for an article of manufacture may obtain a patent therefor, subject to the conditions and requirements of this title.

The provision of this title relating to patents for inventions shall apply to patents for designs, except as otherwise provided.

§ 172. *Right of priority*

The right of priority provided for by section 119 of this title * and the time specified in section 102 (d) shall be six months in the case of designs.

§ 173. *Term of design patent*

Patents for designs may be granted for the term of three years and six months, or for seven years, or for fourteen years, as the applicant, in his application, elects.

* This relates to earlier filings abroad.

Appendix C

Recommendations of the President's Commission on the Patent System

The President's Commission on the Patent System was appointed by President Lyndon B. Johnson on April 8, 1965, "to insure that the patent system will be more effective in serving the public interest." The co-chairmen were Dr. Harry Huntt Ransom, chancellor of the University of Texas, and Simon H. Rifkind, a New York lawyer. On November 17, 1966, the Commission made its report, embodying more than thirty recommendations. President Johnson transmitted to Congress on February 21, 1967, a bill called the Patent Reform Act of 1967, which was based on the recommendations. The bill did not pass, but some of the recommendations may yet be adopted.

Recommendations I to XXXV are reproduced below—grouped under the nine general headings used in the commission's final report—except for recommendation XXXII, which was to have been on government patent policy. (The commission decided not to consider this subject.) The complete report contains much material elaborating the recommendations. As of this writing, copies were still available from the Superintendent of Documents, U.S. Government Printing Office, under the title *"To Promote the Progress of . . . Useful Arts"* in an Age of Exploding Technology.

PATENTABILITY OF INVENTIONS

I. Prior art shall comprise any information, known to the public, or made available to the public by means of disclosure in tangible form or by use or placing on sale, anywhere in the world, prior to the effective filing date of the application. A disclosure in a U.S. patent or published complete application shall constitute prior art as of its effective (U.S. or foreign) filing date.

II. A preliminary application may be used to secure a filing date for all features of an invention disclosed therein, if the disclosure subsequently appears in a complete application. Requirements as to form shall be minimal and claims need not be included. One or more preliminary applications may be consolidated into one complete application filed within twelve months of the earliest preliminary or foreign application relied on.

III. Prior art shall not include, as to the inventor concerned, disclosures of an invention resulting from: (1) a display in an official or officially recognized international exhibition; or (2) an unauthorized public divulgation of information derived from the inventor.

IV. The classes of patentable subject matter shall continue as at present, except: (1) all provisions in the patent statute for design patents shall be deleted, and another form of protection provided; (2) all provisions in the patent statute for plant patents shall be deleted, and another form of protection provided; (3) a series of instructions which control or condition the operation of a data processing machine, generally referred to as a "program," shall not be considered patentable regardless of whether the program is claimed as: (a) an article, (b) a process described in terms of the operations performed by a machine pursuant to a program, or (c) one or more machine configurations established by a program.

APPLICATION FILING AND EXAMINATION

V. (1) Either the inventor or assignee may file and sign both the preliminary and complete applications. Any application filed by the assignee shall include a declaration of ownership at the time of filing and, prior to publication of the application, shall include a declaration of originality by the inventor and evidence of a recorded specific assignment. (2) Every application shall include, at the time of filing, the name of each person believed to have made an inventive contribution. (3) Omission of an inventor's name or inclusion of the name of a person not an inventor, without deceptive intent, shall not affect validity, and can be corrected at any time.

VI. Claim for a priority date must be made when a complete application is filed.

VII. Publication of a pending application shall occur eighteen to twenty-four months after its earliest effective filing date, or promptly after allowance or appeal, whichever comes first. An applicant, for any reason, may request earlier publication of his pending complete application. An application shall be "republished" promptly after allowance or appeal subsequent to initial publication, and again upon issuance as a patent, to the extent needed to update the initially published application and give notice of its status.

VIII. Unless a later filed application is: (1) a continuation application and is filed before the occurrence of any of the following events: (a) the abandonment of, (b) the allowance of all pending claims in, or (c) the filing of an appeal to the Board of Appeals as to any claim in, the original parent application; or (2) a continuation-in-part application and is filed before the publication of any of its parent applications; or (3) a divisional application filed (a) on one of the inventions indicated to be divisible in a restriction requirement and is filed during the pendency of the application in which the restriction was first required, or (b) during the pendency of the original parent application; the later filed application shall not be entitled to the effective filing date of a parent application for matter disclosed in the parent, and the parent, if published, shall constitute prior art against the later filed application.

IX. Statutory authority should be provided for optional deferred examination. An optional deferred examination system shall include the following provisions: (1) The examination shall be deferred at the option of the applicant, exercised by his election not to accompany the complete application with an examination fee. Request for examination, accompanied by payment of an examination fee, may be made anytime within five years from the effective filing date of the application. (2) A deferred application shall be promptly inspected for formal matters and then published. (3) Any party, without being required to disclose his identity, may provoke an examination upon request and payment of the fee. (4) Unless made special upon the request of any party, an application initially deferred shall be inserted in the queue of applications set for examination in an order based on the date of payment of the examination fee. (5) Examination of pending parent or continuing applications shall not be deferred beyond the time when examination is requested of any of the parent or continuing applications.

X. The applicant shall have the burden of persuading the Patent Office that a claim is patentable.

XI. The Patent Office shall consider all patents or publications, the pertinency of which is explained in writing, cited against an application anytime until six months after the publication which gives notice that the application has been allowed or appealed to the Board of Appeals. If the Patent Office, after the citation period, determines that a claim should not be, or have been, allowed, the applicant shall be notified and given an opportunity *ex parte* both to rebut the determination and to narrow the scope of the claim. The identity of the party citing references shall be maintained in confidence. Public use proceedings, as at present, may be instituted during the citation period.

XII. The Patent Office shall develop and maintain an effective control program to evaluate, on a continuing basis, the quality of the patents being issued by the examining groups and art units therein, and to furnish information for the publication of an annual rating of the overall quality of the patents issued each year.

Direct Review of Patent Office Decisions

XIII. A Patent Office decision refusing a claim shall be given a presumption of correctness, and shall not be reversed unless clearly erroneous.

XIV. Either the applicant or the Patent Office may appeal from a decision of the Court of Customs and Patent Appeals to the United States Court of Appeals for the District of Columbia Circuit, and from a decision of the latter court either may petition the Supreme Court for a writ of certiorari.

Procedure for Amending and Cancelling Patents

XV. The Patent Office, upon receipt of a relatively high fee, shall consider prior art of which it is apprised by a third party, when such prior art is cited and its pertinency explained in writing within a three year period after issuance of the patent. If the Patent Office then determines that a claim should not have been allowed, the patent owner shall be notified and given an opportunity *ex parte* both to rebut the determination and to narrow the scope of the claim. Failure to seek review, or the affirmance of the Patent Office holding, shall result in cancellation of the claim. When the validity of a claim is in issue before both the Patent Office and a court, the tribunal where the issue was first presented shall proceed while the other shall suspend consideration, unless the court decides otherwise for good cause. Anyone unsuccessfully seeking Patent Office cancellation of claims shall be required to pay the patent owner's reasonable cost of defending such claims, including attorney's fees. The Commissioner shall require an appropriate deposit or bond for this purpose at the start of the action.

XVI. A claim shall not be broadened in a reissue application.

Liability and Enforcement

XVII. For infringement of a claim which appears in both an application as initially published and in the issued patent, damages may be obtained for an interim period prior to issuance. Such period shall be measured from after the occurrence of all of the following events: (1) the initial publication, (2) a Patent Office holding that the claim is allowable, and (3) a transmittal to the alleged infringer of actual notice resonably indicating how his particular acts are considered to infringe the claim. The applicant's election to create such interim liability, by his transmittal of notice, shall constitute the granting of a reasonable royalty, nonexclusive license, (1) extending only until the issuance of the patent for any infringement involving a process, and (2) extending to and beyond issuance for any infringement involving a machine, manufacture or composition of matter, which is made prior to the issuance of the patent. In exceptional cases, damages for interim infringement up to treble reasonable royalties may be assessed.

XVIII. The term of a patent shall expire twenty years after its earliest effective U.S. filing date.

XIX. The term of a patent, whose issuance has been delayed by reason of the application being placed under secrecy order, shall be extended for a period equal to the delay in issuance of the patent after notice of allowability.

XX. The filing of a terminal disclaimer shall have no effect in overcoming a holding of double patenting.

XXI. The importation into the United States of a product made abroad by a process patented in the United States shall constitute an act of infringement.

XXII. The licensable nature of the rights granted by a patent should be clarified by specifically stating in the patent statute that: (1) applications for patents, patents, or any interests therein may be licensed in the whole, or in any specified part, of the field of use to which the subject matter of the claims of the patent are directly applicable, and (2) a patent owner shall not be deemed guilty of patent misuse merely because he agreed to a contractual provision or imposed a condition on a licensee, which has (a) a direct relation to the disclosure and claims of the patent, and (b) the performance of which is reasonable under the circumstances to secure to the patent owner the full benefit of his invention and patent grant. This recommendation is intended to make clear that the "rule of reason" shall constitute the guidelines for determining patent misuse.

XXIII. A final federal judicial determination declaring a patent claim invalid shall be *in rem,* and the cancellation of such claim shall be indicated on all patent copies subsequently distributed by the Patent Office.

XXIV. Offices of "civil commissioner" shall be created in those U.S. district courts where justified by the volume of patent litigation. In patent cases, unless otherwise ordered by a district court judge for good cause, a commissioner shall conduct pretrial hearings, preside at depositions of parties, supervise discovery proceedings upon an accelerated and abbreviated basis, make preliminary rulings upon the admissibility of proofs, and be empowered to vary the burdens of proof for good cause in secrecy cases.

XXV. A party to a patent case seeking to reduce his litigation costs, with the consent of the adverse party, may submit his case to the court on a stipulation of facts or on affidavits without the usual pretrial discovery. This procedure may be used where no injunctive relief is asked and only limited damages are sought. Incentives shall be provided to consent to this procedure.

STATUTORY ADVISORY COUNCIL

XXVI. A statutory advisory council, comprised of public members selected to represent the principal areas served by the patent system, and appointed by the Secretary of Commerce, shall be established to advise him, on a continuing basis, of its evaluation of the current health of the patent system and, specifically, of the quality of patents being issued and the effectiveness of any internal patent quality control program then in operation, and whether an optional deferred examination system should be instituted or terminated. Every fourth year the council shall publish a report on the condition of the patent system including recommendations for its improvement. The membership shall consist of not less than twelve nor more than twenty-four. The term of appointment shall be four years, with a maximum tenure of eight years. An executive director, and other support as deemed necessary, shall be provided.

PATENT OFFICE OPERATIONS

XXVII. The Patent Office should be supported adequately to insure first-class staffing, housing and equipment, and Patent Office financing should be established on the following basis: (1) The Patent Office should not be required to be entirely self-sustaining. (2) The Commissioner of Patents should be authorized to set fees for Patent Office services within broad guidelines established by

Congress. Such fees shall be apportioned in accordance with the cost of providing the services. (3) The Patent Office should be authorized to establish a "revolving fund" of all its receipts to support its operation.

XXVIII. The applicant should be permitted to amend his case following any new ground of objection or rejection by the Patent Office, except where the new ground of objection or rejection is necessitated by amendment of the application by the applicant.

XXIX. A study group comprising members from industry, technical societies and government should be established to make a comprehensive study of the application of new technology to Patent Office operations and to aid in developing and implementing the specific recommendations which follow. (1) The United States, with other interested countries, should strive toward the establishment of a unified system of patent classification which would expedite and improve its retrieval of prior art. The United States should expand its present reclassification efforts. (2) The Patent Office should be encouraged and given resources to continue, and to intensify, its efforts toward the goal of a fully mechanized search system. (3) The Patent Office should acquire and store machine-readable scientific and technical information as it becomes available. The Patent Office should encourage voluntary submission by patent applicants of copies of their applications in machine-readable form. (4) The Patent Office should investigate the desirability of obtaining the services of outside technical organizations for specific, short-term classification and mechanized search projects.

XXX. The Patent Office should: (1) Proceed vigorously with the implementing of its plan for microform reproduction of all search files; and (2) Cooperate with foreign national patent offices and international patent organizations to develop a worldwide index of patents and published applications for patents.

TRANSITION

XXXI. The legislation implementing the proposed recommendations of the commission should become effective as soon as practical with regard to both patents and pending applications.

INTERNATIONAL ACTION

XXXIII. The United States should take a position in favor of the proposed revision of the Paris Convention whereby a right of priority may be based on an application for an inventor's certificate.

XXXIV. Efforts should be made to have the Paris Convention modified to remove any obstacle to measuring the term of a patent from an effective foreign filing date.

XXXV. The commission believes that the ultimate goal in the protection of inventions should be the establishment of a universal patent, respected throughout the world, issued in the light of, and inventive over, all of the prior art of the world, and obtained quickly and inexpensively on a single application, but only in return for a genuine contribution to the progress of the useful arts. To this end the commission specifically recommends the pursuit of: (1) international harmonization of patent practice, (2) the formation of regional patent system groups, and (3) a universal network of mechanized information storage and retrieval systems.

Appendix D

The Law of Trade Secrets

At a 1969 George Washington University conference, Edgar E. Barton, *a partner in White and Case, a New York law firm, outlined the legal aspects of the loss of trade secrets as follows.**

Trade secret law in the United States is the common law corollary of statutory patent law: the common law aspect of the dual system of American law designed to protect technological ideas. As such the scope of trade secret protection is restricted by the same considerations of policy that confine patent protection to a fixed number of years and to developments of demonstrable originality. Both trade secret and patent law reflect the tension between the objectives of maintaining a free market of ideas on the one hand, and assuring an innovator his rights to enjoy the competitive advantage of his innovation, on the other.

Trade secrets are not limited to a term of years and are not required to meet the same standard of novelty expected of patentable inventions, but trade secret protection is nevertheless in many respects both limited and tenuous. The trade secret owner is protected only against use of his secret by one who has discovered it by unfair means, either by theft, contract violation or

* Reprinted, with permission, from *IDEA,* published by The PTC Research Institute of The George Washington University, Washington, D.C.

by breach of some confidential relationship. He is not protected against anyone else who may independently use or copy his secret.

Moreover, trade secrets are easily lost, for they are protectible only as long as they remain in some degree secret. Once a secret is either discovered independently, or wittingly or unwittingly revealed to someone not in a confidential relationship to the owner of the secret, protection ceases and the owner of the secret finds that he has lost all right to any exclusive use of his innovation. Disclosure may occur through the sale of a product embodying the secret, through publication of the idea in a trade or technical journal, through unprotected use in a foreign country, through disclosure upon issuance of a patent, or through seepage in the course of production or manufacture either to employees or to outsiders who learn of the secret without being under any confidential obligation to the owner of the secret.

I would like to discuss these limits; the ways in which trade secrets can be lost, intentionally or inadvertently.

(1) *Measures to protect secrecy in manufacturing and production plant:*

The very nature of the manufacturing process initially requires that a number of company employees have access to a trade secret, and courts do not require absolute secrecy—they require only reasonable measures to protect secrecy in the light of the circumstances surrounding a particular case.

Thus in *Space Aero Products* v. *R. E. Darling Co.* the Court of Appeals of the State of Maryland carefully balanced the measures taken to protect the secret design of Darling's oxygen breathing hoses against the circumstances of that case. There was evidence on behalf of the owner of the secret that the design had been kept secret from Darling's employees at least during the initial stages of development, that Darling's instruction guide issued for trainees had warned against disclosure and had announced that the design was considered a secret, that the blueprints for the design of the breathing hoses were kept in a locked box access to which was carefully regulated, and that the training of employees with access to the hose design was done in an area separate from the rest of the plant.

On the other hand there was evidence that Darling permitted tours of the plant and public demonstrations of hose assembly, that the production plant's garage doors to the street were frequently left open while hose was being assembled, and that the employees of the plant in general were never cautioned against any disclosure of the hose design. Despite this evidence the court concluded that in the light of the fact that Darling's plant was relatively isolated in a small community, and in the light of the fact that no one had yet succeeded in making hoses according to the Darling process, the precautions taken to preserve secrecy would in these particular circumstances be considered adequate.

In other cases courts may in various circumstances require warning signs, restrictions on outside visitors, maintenance of internal secrecy, control of the number of and qualifications of employees with access to a secret, coding of the names of ingredients, maintenance of plans and documents under lock, repeated admonitions to employees, the destruction of laboratory samples, trash, blueprints, and papers. It is in situations such as the case of *U.S. Plywood Corp.* v. *General Plywood Corp.* (1966), 370 F. 2d 500, that courts will refuse trade secret protection on the ground that plant secrecy has not been maintained. In that case employees were never warned against disclosure. The owner itself made a variety of disclosures to prospective licensees without seeking to impose an obligation of non-disclosure and no special measures were taken to preserve secrecy at the manufacturing plant itself.

(2) Loss through sale of product embodying trade secret:

Undoubtedly the most frequent loss of trade secrets occurs through the marketing, display or advertisement of a product embodying a secret.

Any secret which can be discerned upon examination and inspection of a product or advertisement is lost upon such marketing or advertisement. The same rule applies when such an article is put on display. But courts have distinguished between features of a product which can be ascertained from observation and those which are disclosed only upon dissassembly, chemical analysis or technical investigation. Features revealed only upon analysis are frequently held to remain protectible. In *Extrin Foods, Inc.* v. *Leighton* (Sup. Ct. 1952), 115 N.Y.S. 2d 429, a New York court held that a list of ingredients on the label of a marketed food product did not disclose the secret of the formula used in the manufacture of such product where the list of ingredients did not itemize either the percentages or amounts of each ingredient. Similarly, the classic case of *Tabor* v. *Hoffman*, 118 N.Y. 30 (1889), held that the marketing of a pump did not disclose and destroy the trade secret, defined as the patterns and molds used to manufacture the pump, inasmuch as the specifications of such molds and patterns could be discovered only through reverse engineering from the final product.

But the distinction between apparent features held disclosed upon marketing and those requiring analysis which are held to remain protectible, is neither very clearly defined nor very satisfactory. There are a number of cases finding protectible secrets in already marketed products which candidly emphasize that the gravamen of trade secret recovery is breach of faith. In *Smith* v. *Dravo Corp.*, 203 F. 2d 369 (7th Cir. 1953), the court said: "Pennsylvania will not deny recovery merely because the design could have been obtained through inspection." Rather, the inquiry in that jurisdiction appears to be: How did defendant learn of plaintiff's design? And in *Franke* v. *Wiltschek*, 209 F. 2d 493 (2nd Cir. 1953), the court said:

It matters not that defendants could have gained their knowledge from a study of plaintiffs' publicly marketed product. The fact is that they did not. Instead they gained it from plaintiffs via their confidential relationship and in so doing incurred duty not to use it to plaintiffs' detriment.

The language in these cases and in others suggests that the result in a trade secret case, even where information is publicly available, may depend upon whether the defendant has in fact acquired it through exploitation of a confidential relationship with the owner of the secret. These cases would emphasize that the core of the trade secret cause of action is the tort of unfair competition or unfair misappropriation of the property of another.

(3) *Loss of trade secrets through patent issuance:*

Although trade secret and patent law are in many respects complementary, being two parts of a system designed to encourage innovation, they are nevertheless in some respects potentially in conflict: Patent law offers complete protection for exclusive use of an innovation over a specified period of years in exchange for full public disclosure of the contents of such invention. Trade secret law, on the other hand, requires no disclosure and in fact depends upon the maintenance of secrecy, offering limited protection against unfair misappropriation only so long as an innovation remains confidential and secret.

The owner of an innovation must choose between patent and trade secret protection, for issuance of a patent requires disclosure which itself terminates any prior trade secret protection. Moreover, extended prior trade secret use will preclude later patent application. And issuance of a patent probably destroys all prior competing trade secret claims to the same innovation. A trade secret user may even be liable to a subsequent patentee for infringement.

Patent application—as opposed to actual patent issuance—will not defeat trade secret protection. And trade secrets as to improvements, combinations, uses or adaptations of patented inventions may survive and co-exist with such patents.

Since *Sears* and *Compco,* the Supreme Court unfair competition cases have precluded a state from prohibiting the palming off of copies of an unpatented product. There have been additional suggestions that trade secret law may be preempted by federal patent law. Courts have so far, generally, rejected this suggestion on the ground that trade secret law is limited to protection from unfair misappropriation in violation of a contractual or confidential duty of nondisclosure.

Nonetheless, the relation of patents to trade secrets is one of the most interesting areas of current trade secret development.

Bibliography

Books and Periodicals

APLA Bulletin. American Patent Law Association, Arlington, Va. Monthly.

Berle, Alf K., and L. Sprague de Camp. *Inventions, Patents and Their Management.* Princeton, N.J.: Van Nostrand, 1959.

Calvert, Robert, ed. *The Encyclopedia of Patent Practice and Invention Management.* New York: Reinhold, 1964.

Federico, P. J., ed. *Outline of the History of the United States Patent Office.* Centennial issue of the *Journal of the Patent Office Society,* July, 1936.

IDEA. PTC Research Institute, George Washington University, Washington, D.C. Quarterly, and conference issue.

Jewkes, John, David Sawers, and Richard Stillerman. *The Sources of Invention.* New York: St. Martin's Press, 1958.

Jones, Stacy V. *The Inventor's Patent Handbook.* New York: Dial, rev. ed., 1969.

Journal of the Patent Office Society. Box 685, Washington, D.C., 20044. Monthly.

Patent Trends. National Patent Council, Washington, D.C. Monthly.

Patents of the Week. Newspaper column in Saturday's *New York Times.* (Distributed to other newspapers by the *New York Times* News Service.)

Rossman, Joseph. *Industrial Creativity: The Psychology of the Inventor.* New Hyde Park, N.Y.: University Books, Inc. 1964.

Government Publications
Available from the Patent Office

General Information Concerning Patents.
General Information Concerning Trademarks.

Questions and Answers About Patents.
Questions and Answers About Plant Patents.
Questions and Answers About Trademarks.

Available from the Government Printing Office

Annual Index of Patents.
Annual Index of Trademarks.
Annual Report on Government Patent Policy (Federal Council for Science and Technology).
Commissioner of Patents Annual Report.
Decision Leaflets (from *Official Gazette*). Weekly.
Decisions of the Commissioner of Patents. Annual.
Directory of Registered Patent Attorneys and Agents, Arranged by States and Countries. 1969.
Guide for Patent Draftsmen. Revised periodically.
Manual of Classification. By annual subscription.
Manual of Patent Examining Procedure. By annual subscription.
Official Gazette. Weekly.
Patent Laws. 1965.
Patents and Inventions—An Information Aid to Inventors. Revised periodically.
Patents: Spur to American Progress. 1969.
Rules of Practice of the United States Patent Office in Patent Cases. 1970.
The Story of the United States Patent Office. 1965.
"To Promote the Progress of . . . Useful Arts" in an Age of Exploding Technology (Report of the President's Commission on the Patent System). 1966.
Trademark Rules of Practice of the Patent Office with Forms and Statutes. 1966.
Trademark Supplements (from *Official Gazette*). Weekly.

Committee Prints, Issued by the
Subcommittee on Patents, Trademarks, and Copyrights of the
Senate Committee on the Judiciary

1. *Proposals for Improving the Patent System,* by Vannevar Bush. 1955.
2. *The Patent System and the Modern Economy,* by George Frost. 1956.

3. *Distribution of Patents Issued to Corporations (1939–55)*, by Commissioner Robert C. Watson and P. J. Federico. 1957.
4. *Opposition and Revocation Proceedings in Patent Cases*, by P. J. Federico. 1957.
5. *The International Patent System and Foreign Policy*, by Raymond Vernon. 1957.
6. *Patents and Non-Profit Research*, by Archie M. Palmer. 1957.
7. *Efforts to Establish a Statutory Standard of Invention*, by Victor L. Edwards. 1958.
8. *The Role of the Court Expert in Patent Litigation*, by Leo H. Whinery. 1958.
9. *Recordation of Patent Agreements: A Legislative History*, by Michael Daniels and Victor L. Edwards. 1958.
10. *Exchange of Patent Rights and Technical Information Under Mutual Aid Programs*, by Michael H. Cardozo. 1958.
11. *The Impact of the Patent System on Research*, by Seymour Melman. 1958.
12. *Compulsory Licensing of Patents: A Legislative History*, by Catherine S. Corry. 1958.
13. *Patent Office Fees: A Legislative History*, by Victor L. Edwards. 1958.
14. *Economic Aspects of Patents and the American Patent System* (a bibliography), by Julius W. Allen. 1958.
15. *An Economic Review of the Patent System*, by Fritz Machlup. 1958.
16. *The Research and Development Factor in Mergers and Acquisitions*, by Murray Friedman. 1958.
17. *Renewal Fees and Other Fees in Foreign Countries*, by P. J. Federico. 1958.
18. *Synthetic Rubber: A Case Study in Technological Development Under Government Direction*, by Robert A. Solo. 1959.
19. *Compulsory Licensing of Patents Under Some Non-American Systems*, by Fredrik Neumeyer. 1959.
20. *A Special Court of Patent Appeals: A Legislative History*, by Margaret Conway. 1959.
21. *Technical Research Activities of Cooperative Associations*, by John C. Green. 1959.
22. *Government Assistance to Invention and Research: A Legislative History*, by Barbara H. Jibrin. 1960.
23. *Expediting Patent Office Procedure: A Legislative History*, by Margaret M. Conway. 1960.

24. *Patent and Technical Information Agreements,* U.S. Department of State. 1960.
25. *Court Decisions as Guides to Patent Office,* Patent Office. 1960.
26. *The Patent System—Its Economic and Social Basis,* Treasury Department. 1960.
27. *An Analytical History of the Patent Policy of HEW,* by Gladys A. Harrison. 1960.
28. *Independent Inventors and the Patent System,* by C. D. Tuska. 1961.
29. *The Examination System in the U.S. Patent Office,* by E. W. Geniesse. 1961.
30. *The Law of Employed Inventors in Europe,* by Fredrik Neumeyer. 1962.

Invention and the Patent System, by S. C. Gilfillan. Prepared for the Subcommittee; issued by the Joint Economic Committee of Congress, 1964.

Index